10 center left
Fishermen's houses at Kekova on the Lycian coast, where one sees many sarcophagi, Byzantine fortifications and ruins of cities partly under water because of the slow sinking characteristic of this stretch of the Turkish coastline. The sea is so transparent here that the columns and capitals on the sea bottom can be seen with the naked eye.

10 bottom left
At Kata Kalesi, near Mt. Nemrut and the tomb-mausoleum of Antiochus I, lie the ruins of Yeni Kale (New Fortress), a Mamluk fortress built to defend the interior of Turkey, a region which over the centuries was always subject to raids on the part of invaders from the vast Anatolian plateau.

10-11 Despite the massive efforts made to develop the tourist industry, Turkey's Mediterranean coast still has many perfectly intact spots, such as this beach at Kekova, an island famous for its underwater ruins.

11 top left
The Baglidere valley in Cappadocia is filled with natural "obelisks," tufa needles with bizarre shapes formed by the erosion of the layers of volcanic ash deposited by ancient eruptions.

11 top right
The territory of ancient Lycia is rather rugged, with hills that descend to the sea along a splendid coast, a paradise of crystal-clear water and deserted coves that should be explored by boat.

10 top left
Sunflowers, wheat and cotton are cultivated in vast areas and are the most important and common crops in Turkey. Anatolia, which consists of arid zones unsuitable for farming that alternate with extremely fertile areas, boasts the most intense agricultural activity.

which still permeates Western culture. And what can one say of the splendid and indecipherable calligraphy on the Iznik ceramics, like colored lacework whose inventiveness is codified yet much freer than first meets the eye? Where else can you find a geological phenomenon like the one Mother Nature created in Cappadocia, a vast expanse of needles that offered refuge to shepherds, hermits and monks, who for centuries cut houses, stables, hermitages, monasteries, churches and entire towns out of the rock? Not to mention the petrified falls of Pamukkale, white limescale formations that are unique masterpieces of nature, just as Cappadocia is unique. And then there are the Crusader castles and the caravanserais, the old hostels for the tireless camel caravans that transported goods from one end of Asia and Africa to the other.

Because of its profound aspirations and historic heritage, the soul of Turkey is two-fold. The skyscrapers in Istanbul have not eliminated the old bazaar; the minarets coexist with the crowded beaches; the Anatolian kilims no longer cover the earth under the nomads' tents but now decorate the halls of modern hotels. The contrasts and contradictions within Turkey only serve to increase its appeal, adding an unresolved, impenetrable and uncertain quality to this land. If on the one hand there are now more women with scarves covering their heads and dressed in drab housecoats, on the other hand there are just as

many girls in jeans, especially in the cities, who assert their desire to belong to Western society.

Turkey is incredibly appealing not only because of its scenery and history, but also because the Turks are so positive and optimistic. Leaving aside political events and stances that are as extreme as they are extraneous to the majority of the population, the Turks are dignified, hospitable people. Even in the most remote hamlet in Anatolia, when the bread has just been taken out of the oven, the locals offer some to foreign visitors, together with the apricots left to dry in the sun on the terrace of every home.

The Turks like foreigners, and this has contributed quite a lot to the growth of the local tourist industry, which has become one of the mainstays of the national economy. Accommodation facilities have made great strides in the last two decades to meet the growing demands of tourism. But, here, as elsewhere, mistakes have been made. Excessive and unrestrained building certainly has not helped the landscape, whose past beauty is now only a dim memory. The problem was that everything had to be done hastily to create a network of hotels and residences in record time to compete with Greece, Spain and Italy in order to become one of the leading countries of Mediterranean tourism. But there were, and still are, all the requisites: the sea along the Turkish coast is unpolluted except for those areas of the shoreline

*12 top
The Hellenistic Celsus
Library at Ephesus
was one of the most
important buildings
in this city, which was
quite powerful and a
leading cultural
center.*

*12-13 The sunset
light caresses the
colossal head of Zeus
Oromandes,
photographed from the
east terrace of the
funerary complex of
Antiochus I on Mt.
Nemrut.*

where fishermen's villages have been turned into tourist resorts, and there are stretches that extend for miles with coves and beaches, roadsteads, and gulfs in which the maritime pines almost touch the waves. Fortunately, the coastline is still splendid. The landing places for the caïques appear one after the other, and in the evening the fish in the restaurants couldn't be fresher.

The city of Istanbul, for centuries the symbol of cosmopolitan and multicultural life, deserves a chapter all to itself, since it alone would be enough for one trip.

In the last few decades, this many-faceted and colorful city has been in the throes of a building fever, justified by the ever-growing population (there are now nearly twelve million inhabitants). The other aspect of modern Turkey is the constant attraction that the cities, especially Istanbul, have on country dwellers, who take their entire clan to live in them. At first they make do by living outdoors, then they build temporary houses known as *geçekondo*; the next step is to be assigned a public housing apartment in the boundless outskirts. Istanbul, Ankara and Izmir are still faced with this problem, which in the rest of Europe is becoming less and less critical.

The heart of ancient Byzantium is represented by the historic districts along the shores of the Golden Horn, around Sultanahmet, at Hagia Sophia, and around the Topkapi, the royal palace par excellence. Instead of the palaces of Basra, in Iraq, the *Thousand and One Nights* could well have been set in the fabulous sultans' palace between the Bosporus and the Golden Horn, which evokes rather grim images of harems and odalisques. This is the real Istanbul, which must be visited on foot, through the alleyways, slipping in and out the bazaar, sipping real Turkish coffee in the cool shade of a grapevine pergola far from the noisy, traffic-filled streets.

Although the modernization of the city has continued, there remains some evidence of its fascinating past. For example, the Café of Pierre Loti, the French author madly in love with the East, is still on the Eyüp hill, and though it caters mostly to tourists, it remains open; and Kariye Camii, which was the splendid Byzantine church of St. Saviour in Chora, with the most beautiful mosaics imaginable, is still surrounded by a neighborhood with the last surviving wooden houses, the *yali*. Much has been destroyed and much has been salvaged, from the pleasure pavilions of the last sultans to the gardens whose flowerbeds are overflowing with lale, the tulips that were favorites with

the sovereigns. Then there are incongruous palaces such as Dolmabahçe and Beylerbeyi, built with a Baroque-like pompousness that contrasted so strikingly with the weakness of the last Ottoman rulers, perhaps as a sort of "last stand" of the power of the Sublime Porte, which was declining inexorably. Turkey succeeds in merging, in a logical pattern, the capital of an empire that was pagan, Christian and Muslim with the silent deserted stretches of the Anatolian interior. It somehow harmonizes, without undue contrast, important modern cities like Ankara, the capital that rose again from oblivion to become a copy of the metropolis, or industrialized Bursa, the almost forgotten former Ottoman capital, and cities like Konya, which is a religious center. A lot remains to be discovered in entire areas that are unknown to fast-paced mass tourism, which seems to be interested only in the overcrowded sights. For example, there is the quiet Black Sea, its green coasts dotted with tea and tobacco plantations; Cappadocia, rich in magical and solitary towns and valleys that are every bit as lovely as the localities packed with tourists; the southern coast, where there are still villages where people live by fishing and are blessed with simple hospitality; and Anatolia, a veritable wellspring of archaeological treasures that for some strange reason are off the beaten tourist track, such as Gordium, with the astonishing tumulus tomb of King Midas, and the rock-hewn monasteries in the gorges of the mountains skirting the Black Sea, particularly the Sumela convent. It is therefore rather superficial to limit our knowledge of such a land to only four or five major sights. Turkey deserves much more than this, if only to do justice to her history, which dates back to the dawn of civilization, and to her scenery, which sometimes seems so familiar and at other times so exotic. Turkey is all this and more, much like the scent of spices and the wind that comes from ancient solitary places and merges with the warm Mediterranean breezes. It is a country pulsating with emotions that we simply cannot ignore.

Romania

Black Sea

Bulgaria

• Edirne

Bosporus

Istanbul • Üsküdar   • Sile

Sea
of Marmara

• İzmit

Dardanelles

• Çanakkale

Greece

A e g e a n

• Bursa

• İznik (Nicaea)

Sakarya

Sea

∴ Troy

Bögazkale

Hattusas

Ankara

• Pergamum

Gordium

Lesbos

Chios

Hermus

Lake
Tuz

Lydia

• İzmir ∴ Sardis

Ephesus

∴ Miletus

Maeander

• Pamukkale

Samos

∴ Didyma

Bodrum (Halicarnassus)

Cnidus

Marmaris

Kaunos

• Fethiye

Xanthus

Kalkan

Lycia

Kas

Rhodes

Kastellorizon

Aphrodisias

Perga

Antalya

Myra

Konya

Aspendos

• Side

Alanya

Crete

Mediterranean

Sea

Cyprus

Cappadocia: the "Fairies' Chimneys"

The Aegean Sea coast

Russia

Georgia

Azerbaijan

Armenia

s

m o u n t a i n   r a n g e

· Hopa

· Trabzon

Ağri · ▲ Mt.
Ararat
(Ağri Daği)

West Euphrates

Iran

East Euphrates

ocia

Kayseri
·
Göröme Valley
▲ Erciyas Daği

Lake
Van

· Van

∴
Derinkuyu

Nemrut
Daǧ ▲
Euphrates

∴ Zeugma

· Adana

· Iskenderun

Iraq

· Antioch

Mt. Nemrut: the tomb of Queen
Karakus

The Marble Court at Sardis

Syria

The history of Turkey has been a continuous alternation of dazzling grandeur and distressing decline, with no long-lasting periods of tranquil normality, but it has undoubtedly helped to animate and enrich European history. It began long ago, in the obscurity of prehistoric times that will never be totally revealed to us and that strikes its roots in hypothesis, in legend not always backed by facts, in myths, and in the unknown.

The mystery enveloping the dawn of this great country makes it even more fascinating for those who want to get to know and understand it, because the underground cities in Cappadocia are still inexplicable, as are the stylized images of deities–so evocative and disturbing–found in the

18 left This headless image of the voluptuous goddess of fertility comes from a major archaeological site, Çukurkent. Made of polished limestone, the statuette dates back to the third millennium B.C. It is in the Ashmolean Museum, Oxford.

18 bottom An anthropomorphic vase dating from 5500 B.C. and found by a group of British archaeologists at Hacilar, a noteworthy urban settlement in prehistoric Anatolia. This city, built near a spring, comprised nine archaeological levels, from the late Neolithic to the early Chalcolithic ages.

18-19 The first inhabitants of Anatolia were shepherds and hunters. The latter can be seen in this rock painting, a skillfully rendered hunting scene found during excavations at Çätal Hüyük and now kept in the Museum of Anatolian Civilizations, Ankara.

depths of this land. The Anatolian culture gave rise to one of the first civilizations recognized as such, located in the heart of a peninsula that served as a "platform" connecting Europe and Asia like a huge bridge. From the depths of the Palaeolithic era there emerged Çatal Hüyük, which vies with Proto-Palestinian cities such as Jericho as the most ancient urban settlement in the world, since it had a sedentary population that was able to make pottery, executed frescoes and graffiti, cultivate land, raise livestock, weave, and live in communities that performed rites and ceremonies involving particular deities: the Mother Goddess and the Bull, both symbols of fertility. Çatal Hüyük dates back to 7000 B.C., while 5000 B.C. marks the foundation of Hacılar, an archaeological site whose abundance of clay and copper artifacts have led scholars to link it with a more advanced cultural level, the same found in the first archaeological strata in Troy by Schliemann. This was the period in which history crosses the threshold separating the Stone Age from the Bronze Age, when the Anatolian societies were ruled by shepherd-kings and there were self-sufficient urban communities with a network of trade relations with the Mesopotamian populations and, perhaps, even with Egypt.

In this remote age this state of affairs was dealt a violent jolt by the invasion of the Hittites, who settled at Hattushash, present-day Bögazkale, not far from Kayseri, in Cappadocia. The Hittites spoke an Indo-European language, but their origins are still unknown. But despite their overwhelming military power their supremacy in Asia Minor was short-lived. From 1600 B.C. on the Hittite empire expanded to take in the territories now corresponding to Syria, Jordan and Israel, which they conquered from Egypt. In fact, the pharaohs, especially Ramesses II, feared that Hittite pressure would unseat them from their throne.

The Hittites had cuneiform writing, which was deciphered thanks to the clay tablets found at Bögazkale and other localities. They also produced pottery, statuettes, jewels, iron weapons and tools, bas-reliefs and sumptuous buildings. The reasons behind their rapid and irreversible decline are hypothetical at best; according to one credible theory, at the beginning of the second millennium B.C. the Anatolian coasts were over-

20

20 Bas-relief
portraying a Hittite
prince found in
Carchemish and
dating from the
beginning of the
Hittite period.

21 left The thin,
pensive goddess-mother
of Hasanoglen is
embellished with gold
leaf and two heavy
anklets. It dates from
2600-1900 B.C.

21 bottom This first
millennium B.C. bas-
relief from the major
Hurrite city of
Urartu, in the Lake
Van area, shows a
marked Babylonian
influence.

21 center Although
the history of the
Hittites is still partly
wrapped in mystery,
we do know that they
spoke an Indo-
European language
and had a form of
cuneiform script.
This large tile
illustrates the life
of King Katuvas.

run by a wave of invaders from the northeast, perhaps the Dorians – also known as Achaeans – who with their campaign of conquest, which began with the conquest of Troy, brought the evolution of this region to a sudden halt. So it seems that Homer was telling the truth and was thus the first chronicler in history.

In those times the Anatolian plateau could have been considered a veritable *melting pot*, given all the various ethnic groups that lived there: the Hurrites, who settled in the southeastern area of Lake Van and their relatives, who founded the Mitanni kingdom (from which the Aramaic language derived) in the regions bordering present-day Syria; the Carians on the coast, together with the Lycians; and lastly, the Phrygians. The last-mentioned population, which originated in Thrace, subdued almost all the western and central areas. Their capitals were Midas Sehir (the City of Midas, now Yazilikaya) and Gordium. This latter was named

after one of its kings, the father of Midas, the sovereign with fabulous riches. Gordius is known for having made the legendary knot that no one was able to untie until Alexander the Great cut it with a blow of his sword. The tomb of King Midas was found intact at Yassihöyük, but ironically enough, not even an ounce of gold was in it. The ancient Greek historian Herodotus narrates the destiny of the Phrygians, who had to succumb to the umpteenth horde of invaders, this

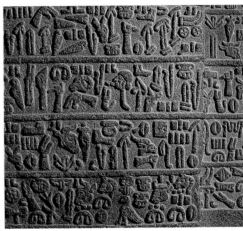

22 A Ptolemaic period alabaster head of Alexander the Great, the Macedonian conqueror who spread Hellenic culture through the coastal areas of Turkey.

22-23 This famous mosaic found in Pompey illustrates the Battle of Issus, the first step in the inexorable advance of Alexander the Great's troops in Asia Minor, which swept over Darius' Persian army.

time the Cimmerians, who were in turn supplanted by the Lydians. These latter founded the city of Sardis, the capital of their last king, Croesus, who is to be considered the first numismatist in history, since the invention of minting dates from his time.

During this period the long coastline, rich in natural landing places and with a hospitable hinterland, witnessed the flourishing of splendid commercial Greek city-states, the self-sufficient *poleis* that proved to be so decisive a factor in the fabric of Hellenic unity that for centuries the Turkish coast was part and parcel of Greek territory and culture.

Besides being prosperous thanks to sea and land trade and to flourishing agriculture, these cities were major cultural nerve centers: two of their leading figures were the philosopher and mathematician Thales, who was born in Miletus, and Eudoxus of Cnidus, an astronomer, physician and mathematician.

In this pleiad of kingdoms and potentates, of populations that declined and others that rose to power, there burst upon the scene the passion for conquest of Cyrus the Great, king of the Persians, whose army started off

from Persepolis, routing the Lydians and taking Croesus prisoner in 546 B.C. Upon Cyrus' death, his successors Darius and Xerxes continued his policy of expansion. Persian dominion was harsh and unbearable due to its violence and the burdensome taxes it imposed, so much so that the local populations never stopped resisting them with every means at their disposal. Then, like a thunderbolt, in 334 B.C. Alexander the Great crossed the Hellespont, initiating the most rapid and astounding series of military victo-

ries in all human history, the main stages of which were the triumphs over the Persians at the Granicus River in 334 and at Issus in 333 B.C.

More than a mere military conquest, Alexander's rise marked a turning point for the fate of Asia Minor, since the true epoch-making victor was Greek civilization itself, as Hellenism permeated the coastal cities definitively and spread to those in the interior. Greek became the official language; theaters, schools, gymnasiums, aqueducts, libraries, temples and

defensive walls were built; and the arts and sciences flourished as never before. The epicenter of the penetration and spread of Greek culture were precisely the cities of Asia Minor, which had trade relations with the entire known world.

Alexander's unexpected and untimely death marked the collapse of his vision of a unified empire. The Macedonian died at Babylon in 323 B.C. and soon afterward his generals began to partition the lands he had conquered, in an atmosphere marked

24 left Detail from the Gate of Herakles (Hercules) at the archaeological site of Ephesus, one of the largest and most ancient in Turkey.

by an infinite series of intrigues, struggles and skirmishes. One of Alexander's generals, Lysimachus, was killed by another one, Seleucus, the ruler of Antioch (now Antakya) and founder of the Seleucid dynasty, in the battle of Corupedion. Seleucus was then eliminated by Ptolemy Ceraunus. In this constellation of thrones and relative domains, the last to arrive were the Galatians, a tribe of mercenaries of Celtic origin hired by the king of Bithynia: these newcomers founded yet another kingdom, Galatia, whose capital was Ancyra, today's Ankara.

In the meantime, the Lake Van region was settled by the Armenians, a Phrygian population that later on enjoyed a period of splendor during the reign of Tigranes I, around 90 B.C. On the coasts of the Black Sea, known as the land of Pontus at that time, Mithridates I ruled at Trebizond around 300 B.C. The most important of these monarchies was the one at Pergamum–which became powerful in 250 B.C.–under the Attalid dynasty, which thwarted the expansionist aims of the Galatians. Thanks to Attalus III, the long period of Roman domination began in Turkey. While dying, this monarch, who had made Pergamum a cultural center with the creation of the huge library, bequeathed his city-state to Rome, thus opening the doors of Asia Minor to this rising power. In fact, the Roman conquest of all Anatolia was not difficult. One obstacle was the opposition of Mithridates VI Eupator, who was defeated in more than one battle by Sulla and Pompey. This latter is also to be credited for having eliminated piracy along the coast.

Julius Caesar dismantled the power of Mithiadates, who had committed suicide rather than be taken prisoner, with the defeat of Pharnaces, Mithradates' son, at Zela. On that occasion Caesar uttered his famous statement, "Veni, vidi, vici" (I came, I saw, I conquered). To consolidate their position, the Romans also confronted the army of the Seleucid king Antiochus III at Magnesia. Overwhelmed by military power, many minor sovereigns pledged loyalty to the new conquerors, and the *Pax Romana* brought peace and prosperity. The Roman administration of these lands was constructive, and both agriculture and trade developed. The Anatolian plateau, the infinite expanses of which had been traversed until then only by shepherds and nomads, was rich in fertile land which began to yield excellent harvests, as did every good plot of land along the Black Sea coast. The Romans loved this vast and surprising province, where sophisticated cities with Hellenistic culture coexisted with wild steppes and mountain chains. Mark Antony and Cleopatra frequented the coast and chose Antakya as the venue of their marriage, and Augustus made Ancyra (Ankara) a major city.

24 right The wealth of Sardis was displayed in the city's impressive public works as well as in the refined decorative motifs in this polychrome marble panel.

25 top A Thracian warrior in battle gear protecting his face with a large shield on a marble funerary stele that was erected by Ammias in memory of her husband Antaios.

25 bottom The city of Sardis was founded by the Lydians and became the capital of their last king, Croesus, a personage described in many legends. In reality he should be considered the first numismatist since he was responsible for some of the most ancient historically documented coins. Shown here is a detail of the Marble Court in Sardis.

In time, however, this idyll was interrupted by various events. In 258 A.D. the Goths razed Anatolia, while in the 280s the Persians, from the east, crossed the borders and overran the Roman territory. Faced respectively by the emperors Claudius II and Diocletian, these two threats were averted, but something much more subtle and long-lasting was looming over the horizon of Rome's glory: the spread of Christianity. This new religion was inexorable despite the Romans' infamous and extremely cruel repression, and soon undermined the credibility of the *imperial establishment*.

The preaching of Saint Paul, who was born in Tarsus, in Cilicia, disseminated Christ's message with extraordinary speed. Paul proselytized through southern Turkey and along the coast, and gave his famous sermon at Ephesus. According to legend, the Apostle John also retired to Ephesus together with Mary, the mother of Jesus; their presumed house lies a short distance from the archaeological precinct.

When Diocletian abdicated, the imperial throne was eventually taken over by Constantine the Great who, realizing that it was impossible to maintain the territory of the Empire as it was during its heyday, took a bold step, moving the capital to Byzantium, the New Rome, which was renamed Constantinople. The emperor continued to amaze his conservative subjects by converting to Christianity and then making it the state religion. Not content with this, in 325 Constantine convened the Council of Nicaea in order to stifle potential heresy and purge Christianity of doctrines that led believers astray from the true path indicated by Christ. The Council abolished Arianism, while the profession of the Christian faith was codified in the Nicene Creed.

In the midst of such fervor there was the spread of hermits, anchorites

and visionaries, who were on the borderline between mad fanaticism and sublimated spirituality and who decided to live in solitude to meditate, practice chastity and mortify their flesh; others chose to preach in order to increase the number of converts. Cappadocia was an ideal place for these "madmen of God" to follow their calling, and the region witnessed the foundation of communities of monks who lived in the caves so characteristic of this land.

At the same time, paganism was doomed. The temples were abandoned and sacked, the images and statues of the pagan gods were destroyed or mutilated. Yet some cults managed to survive in secret; one of these was Mithraism. In the meantime, Justinian had been crowned at Constantinople. This tenacious and ambitious ruler had managed to reconquer part of the Byzantine dominions in Italy from the Goths and 'after becoming emperor' gained new victories in the Balkans, North Africa and Anatolia. Justinian and his vainglorious and strong-minded wife Theodora beautifed the capital with monuments and other large-scale public works, the most splendid of which was the Hagia Sophia basilica. Justinian was also a much appreciated jurist, while his severe tax measures certainly did not make him popular with his subjects. A short time after his death the Lombards again drove the Byzantines from Italy.

Exactly five years separate Justinian's death and the birth of Muhammad in Mecca. This was an event of great importance, marking the rise of Islam, the religion that unified the many Arab tribes.

In the meantime other barbarians invaded the Turkish peninsula–the Avars, Slavs and many other ethnic groups–while toward the southwestern border the Persians resumed their march of conquest. And court life in Constantinople was marked by grim episodes of intrigues, regicide and corruption. This decadence became irresistible, capturing the impotent and faint-hearted cultured class in its snare.

26-27 The Council of Nicaea was basic to the codification of the Christian religion. This mosaic in the SS Quattro Coronati church in Rome shows the Emperor Constantine handing to Pope Sylvester the tiara symbolizing the temporal power given to the head of the Church.

27 bottom A detail of one of the most famous Byzantine mosaics, which dates from the 6th century A.D. and adorns the marvelous San Vitale church in Ravenna. In the middle is Justinian, richly dressed and with an aureole around his crowned head. The emperor is flanked by archibishop Maximian, general Belisarius and court officials.

28-29 The Crusades were characterized by both glorious and disgraceful events. The army of knights and adventurers went to the Near East, conquering cities and building castles on the lands taken from the Muslims. Above is a miniature depicting the conquest of Antioch.

The only positive, albeit not decisive, event in this period was the emperor Heraclius' victory over the Persians in 628.

The invasion of Anatolia on the part of the Muslim Arabs became definitive in 654, when, after capturing Ankara, they laid siege to Constantinople for four years (but did not manage to take it because of the massive walls that Theodosius II had built - part of which are still standing in the heart of Istanbul). However, the Arabs won one victory after the other in the rest of the country.

In the name of Allah and his prophet Muhammad, in the regions under Arab dominion the language, religion and writing of the new rulers was imposed on the locals. Islamic proselytism was both rapid and convincing; one of the arguments used to make converts was that non-believers would have to pay taxes, while the new believers would be exempt.

This was the period of the bizarre crusade against the artistic reproduction of human images for religious worship known as iconoclasm: the images of Christ, the Virgin Mary, the saints and angels were therefore effaced, scraped and otherwise violently removed from the marvelous frescos, mosaics and wood panel paintings that

the Byzantine civilization had produced. At Constantinople the fanatical dispute between the iconclasts and their opponents ended with the victory of human representation in sacred images, thus guaranteeing the survival of great masterpieces for posterity.

Extremely cruel palace intrigues, betrayal and blood-filled crimes became more and more common, but did not prevent the Byzantines from obtaining the occasional victory in their constant, exhausting effort to maintain the borders of the empire. In the 990s Basil II even managed to reconquer part of the land that the Arabs had taken. But it was during this period the Crusaders, on their way to Jerusalem on the Fourth Crusade to liberate the Holy Sepulcher, added insult to injury: they arrived in Constantinople in 1204 and distinguished themselves by the shameful plunder of the city and the horrendous massacre of their fellow Christians.

29 top The Crusaders defended Constantinople from the Muslim assault, but they then sacked and devastated the capital of the Eastern Roman Empire. This miniature, from the 13th-century codex Las Cantigas de Santa Maria, *now kept in the Escorial Library, in Spain, represents the Ottoman attack.*

29 bottom The Vacant Throne of Constantinople, *in a miniature from the Greek manuscript* The Oracle of Leon the Wise *kept in the National Library, Palermo, is an allegory of the defeat of the Ottomans by the Christians.*

This was the muddled, complex and war-torn situation that set the stage for the appearance of the Seljuks, to whom Turkish history owes moments of incomparable splendor and abysmal decadence. But who were the Seljuks in reality? They were a nomad population that arrived in Central Asia sometime before 800 A.D., then settled at Isfahan, in Persia, where they embraced Islam. First-rate soldiers, they were used as mercenaries by the Abbasid caliph al-Mutasim, becoming the mainstay of his army. In fact, they were indispensable for the caliphate and in a short time became the actual rulers of the Abbasid empire. This proud and fierce race enjoyed an innumerable series of military victories. In the battle against the Byzantines at Manzikert they actually captured the emperor Romanus IV. Their triumphal march seemed to be irresistible. But no sooner did they move their capital from Isfahan to Nicaea that they had to face the threat of the devastating Mongol armies led by Genghis Khan, who belonged to the same ethnic group as the Seljuks. The encounter at Sivas was terrible, ending in the defeat of the Seljuks. When all hope seemed to be lost, the unpredictable Mongols, who had arrived so wildly and rapidly, just as inexplicably and rapidly went back to their steppes.

It was then that Ertugrul, a small Seljuk feudal landowner, began to unify once again what had been his people's territory before the arrival of the Mongol "whirlwind." His son Osman, known as Gazi, or "warrior of the faith," successfully continued his father's mission in life. 1288 is the year that marked the birth of Osman I's empire, also known as the Ottoman Empire. The first move was the conquest of Bursa and then of Adrianopolis (Edirne) in Thrace, a city in a key strategic position for control of the Balkans. Osman's son Orkhan continued his father's policy of Ottoman supremacy, both by means of arms and diplomacy. In fact, he married Theodora, the daughter of the pretender to the throne of Constantinople. The wise and moderate Orkhan, a military man but also an able statesman, was succeeded by his son Murad I, who was more impetuous and bellicose. He set out to expand his reign to include the Balkans, thinking that this task would be relatively easy since the Ottomans had moved their capital to Adrianopolis, that is, to European soil. It was in this period, in the mid-1300s, that the Ottoman sultans' elite corps, the famous Janissaries, were founded.

30 bottom left
A gold- and silver-plated copper vase made by artisans in the court of the sultan Orkhan in 1330. In compliance with the Islamic religion, human representations such as this one became less and less frequent and then disappeared altogether.

30 center top, center bottom and right
These miniatures portray three of the sultans who ruled during the golden age of the Ottoman Empire: Osman I, Orkhan and Murad I. A great number of crimes were committed in the sultans' splendid Topkapi palace, but there was also a musical and artistic culture that had a lasting impact on Turkish life. The miniatures are now in the Stapleton Collection.

31 bottom
The famous Louvre Museum in Paris is now the home of this lovely Seljuk ceramic bottle (ca. 1300) in imitation Chinese celadon style; the characteristic greenish-blue glaze is embellished with finely wrought gold elements.

31 right A miniature in a 13th-century edition of Marco Polo's Book of Marvels *(Bibliothèque Nationale, Paris) representing the first journey to Constantinople made by Marco's father and uncle, Nicolò and Matteo Polo, who are portrayed being received by Emperor Baldwin I.*

32 In this miniature (ca. 1720) the pleasures of the harem *are* depicted in a rather chaste manner. The sultan is Ahmed III.

33 center left Oriental influences are clearly seen in the mounts used here, Bactrian camels, which were widespread only in Central Asia.

33 bottom left The Mongol hordes dealt a severe blow to Islamic expansionist aims. Tamerlane's troops conquered the sultans' territory and imposed feudal rule there. An equestrian battle is depicted in this 15th-century miniature.

33 right Sultan Murad II ruled from 1421 to 1451. Ottoman miniatures always show the sultans in a meditative mood, such as when they are smelling flowers or admiring jewels.

These soldiers were the sons of Christians who were forced to convert to Islam. At a tender age they were taken from their families and were trained with harsh and even cruel methods, so it was only natural they would become ruthless and bloodthirsty, arousing terror wherever they went.

Murad I partly realized his expansionist aims by conquering large areas in the Balkans and moving quite far to the west, but he was killed by a Slav in the land he had just won for his empire. Yildirim Beyazid (Beyazid I), known as the Thunderbolt, ascended the throne after Murad and established the horrible tradition of the new sultan strangling to death his brothers or oth-

er pretenders to the throne who might jeopardize the stability of the empire. Beyazid was also the sultan who in 1396 inflicted a terrible and definitive defeat on the knights of the last Crusade. At that favorable moment for the Ottoman Empire he also planned to take Constantinople, but was sidetracked by the arrival of a new enemy, Tamerlane, who was also a Mongol.

Timur Leng, which is his non-Latinized name, went to the aid of some of his vassals in Anatolia who were threatened by the invasions of Beyazid, who had become drunk with delusions of grandeur after his victories in the Balkans. The Ottoman sultan suffered a crushing defeat, and even his invincible Janissaries were exterminated by the fury of the Mongols. The sultan was taken prisoner and so humiliated that he chose to commit suicide. In his thirst for vengeance, Tamerlane eliminated all traces of Beyazid's reign and the four sons of his bitter enemy became his vassals. However, the Mongol conqueror's death triggered a fratricidal feud among the Ottoman heirs, which ended with the victory of Mehmet I, whose son Murad II restored the empire to the splendor known before Beyazid's defeat, while Mehmet II conquered Constantinople in 1453, winnig the name of Muhammad the Conqueror.

Mehmet thus brought Byzantinm's Palaeologian dynasty to an end and, what is more, eliminated the last bulwark of what remained of the Eastern Roman Empire, hoisting the flag of Islam over the former Christian capital.

The day after the Ottomans captured the imperial city they changed its name to Istanbul. The valorous and hopeless defense of Constantinople was led by the Venetian Giovanni Giustiniani, but his heroism and that of his men was in vain: the emperor Constantine XI was the last Christian sovereign to wear the crown that boasted more history, splendor and misdeeds than any other. While all this was taking place outside and in-

side the city walls built by Theodosius, life in the rest of the vast Anatolian plateau, with its pastoral rhythm and primeval rites, continued as always, almost as if the people were unaware of the bloody battle in Constantinople and the momentous change that would result in the political and social history of Eastern Europe.

About seventy years after the conquest of Constantinople, now Istanbul, prince Süleyman, better known as Süleyman the Magnificent, became the sultan of the Ottoman Empire. In that period the power of the Janissaries had exceeded all reasonable limits and their arrogance made life in the court almost unbearable. During his 46 years on the throne, Süleyman's rule was marked by both wisdom and cruelty, culture and intrigue, tolerance and repression. In the meantime the other major thrones of Europe were occupied by sovereigns who left their mark on the destiny of their people and the entire continent. And in the easternmost part of Europe, and the least "European" capital, Istanbul, a true golden age was about to begin, perhaps the first period of magnificence and Islamic humanism that had ever been consolidated under a ruler whose behavior was characterized by many bright as well as dark moments.

A man of great intelligence and foresight, Süleyman aimed at giving the people in his great empire just laws and codified principles that would be administered so as to protect them from oppression and injustice; above

34 *Not all the sultans liked the idleness and pleasures of the court. In fact, some were valorous warriors and able strategists. In this miniature Süleyman the Magnificent is on the front line during the battle of Mohács.*

35 *bottom left Special treatment was reserved for infidels and those who opposed the sultan's wishes, as can be seen in this miniature (1566), in which two European ambassadors are taken prisoner by Süleyman the Magnificent.*

all, he wanted them to be aware that the law was the law precisely because it had to be observed. However, as is obvious, in this great ruler's mind the people had to abide by these ethical precepts, while he himself could ignore them; in fact, many a time in his private life Süleyman deviated from the very morals he himself had promulgated.

The sultan's many victories on the field bore proof of his great prowess as a military strategist. In 1529 the Ottoman armies advanced as far as the outskirts of Vienna, but never managed to conquer the city. However, they did occupy and dominate the Balkan states, Hungary, Greece, all North Africa, Sudan, Somalia and Ethiopia. Syria, Jordan, Lebanon, Palestine, Kuwait, Saudi Arabia, Persia and Iraq were also easily conquered, and the Ottoman power reached its height in this period.

As is natural, the European powers were terrorized by this tempestuous

and seemingly invincible march of conquest. But it came to an end, because Süleyman wanted nothing more to do with European affairs and thus shelved his plans for other wars. Having laid aside his scimitar, the sultan became a patron of art, music and literature and the leading artists and intellectuals in the Ottoman Empire and Europe frequented his court in Istanbul. The precious miniatures that brought fame to the Ottoman period for their elegance, fine details and grace, were painted in this period. The great architect Sinan, originally a Christian who converted to Islam and who designed the most extraordinary mosques in the Muslim world, was patronized by Süleyman, who had him build palaces, bridges and *madrasas* (Islamic theological schools). Istanbul became a beautiful city at this time and the sultan's court was called the Sublime Porte.

35 *top right Istanbul, known as the "Gate to the East," in a miniature from Matrakji's* The Journey. *The work renders in a stylized manner the geographic features of the area, and the vessels at the bottom indicate the importance of the city's port.*

35 *center right The Ottoman Empire was at the height of its expansion when this map was drawn in the early 1600s by Jodocus Hondius for Mercator's* Atlas, *which underscores the vastness of the Sublime Porte's territory.*

Artisans also had the opportunity to show their ability in creating works of artistic worth: wooden and pearl inlay, jewelry, fine repoussé metalwork, silk weaving, painted majolica, lead-alloyed glassware, and finely decorated weapons. Trade flourished, both by sea and via the caravans that came from Africa, Persia and India. The port of Istanbul was considered the busiest and most prosperous in the world at that time.

Süleyman also patronized poets and authors, astronomers and scholars, which led historians to say that the reign of this ruler was a true Renaissance for the Ottoman Empire. However, all this luxury and cultural ferment could not cancel the extent of the crimes committed in the royal court. Süleyman's greatest misdeed was caused by a woman, the sultan's favorite in the large *harem*, Roxelana, who was of European origin. She was the one who initiated the female intrigues that was to play such a major role in the decisions and destiny of the sultans, from Süleyman onward. Roxelana, rechristened Hürrem, had one son from the sultan, Selim, who was mentally retarded. Despite this, in order to secure the throne for him, she did not hesitate to incite Süleyman to kill his two eldest sons, Mustafa and Beyazid, who were the

rightful heirs to the Ottoman throne.

Besides the grim intrigues contrived in the secrecy of the *harem*, life in the Topkapi, the splendid royal palace built by Muhammad the Conqueror, was upset by the revolts of the Janissaries and their reactionary fanaticism. After Süleyman's death they became so bold that they even went so far as to kidnap a sultan, Osman III. All this, added to a total rejection of all technological innovations from Europe, brought about a slow decline, as the empire maintained its feudal system. One example of this reactionary stance is the fact that the introduction of printing in Turkey was obstructed with every means at hand, when it had already been widespread for a quarter century in Europe.

The Istanbul court was considered depraved and barbarous for certain

36 bottom left
Sultan Muhammad II, who ruled from the Sublime Porte in the second half of the 15th century, is portrayed while smelling a flower. The many details in Ottoman miniatures afford accurate documentation of the dress of that time.

36 top right
Sultan Beyazid underestimated the miltary skill of the Mongol invaders and was even taken prisoner during a battle and was then humiliated by his enemy Tamerlane, as can be seen in this miniature dating from the second half of the 17th century.

36-37 This 18th-century painting, kept in the Topkapi palace, shows that the Receptions at the court of Süleyman III were held in the magnificent Audience Hall, known as the Az Odasi.

amoral incidents that took place there. The last straw was the massacre ordered by Mehmet III, who had all his nineteen brothers assassinated for fear that one of them might plot against him and remove him from the throne. In order to avoid universal condemnation of such acts, Ahmed I decided not to suppress potential rivals but to imprison them for life in a jail known as the Golden Cage, from which it was

37 top The Topkapi Saray palace in Istanbul is the subject of this miniature from a 17th-century manuscript kept in the Correr Museum, Venice. The illustration shows the characteristic architectural features of the palace—the many domes and minarets.

absolutely impossible to escape. As can be seen, the customs in the Ottoman Empire were anything but compatible with those in European countries.

In the meantime, besides normal sea trade, the Mediterranean was becoming the venue for Ottoman piracy. The most famous Ottoman corsair was Piri Reis, a man determined to do anything to get hold of booty. The Venetian Republic, the eternal enemy of the Turks and an ally of Spain and the Papal States in the Holy League, decided to put an end to these provocations. At first the Christian fleet was defeated in the battle of Famagusta,

off the Cyprus coast, but it got sweet and splendid revenge at the famous Battle of Lepanto, a crushing victory that virtually destroyed the Turkish fleet for ever. The same fate befell the Turkish army when it was routed in 1683 outside the gates of Vienna during the Ottomans' final attempt to defeat the Hapsburg Empire. With this defeat, the nightmare of the Turkish threat no longer haunted the European people and rulers, while the legend of the Ottomans' invincibility was disproved time and again.

Another fundamental cause of the decline of the Ottoman Empire was

the change in the flow of international trade triggered by the discovery of America and the opening of new routes to India and the Far East, also the result of exploration. Istanbul and Turkey were no longer the obligatory stopping point for communication with the East, and the fabulous Gate of the Orient lost its centuries-old monopoly as the crossroads of the world. This marked a change in the Europeans' attitude as well: the former fear of Ottoman Turkey began to be replaced by curiosity in its lifestyle, which was so utterly different from, and incompatible with, their way of life.

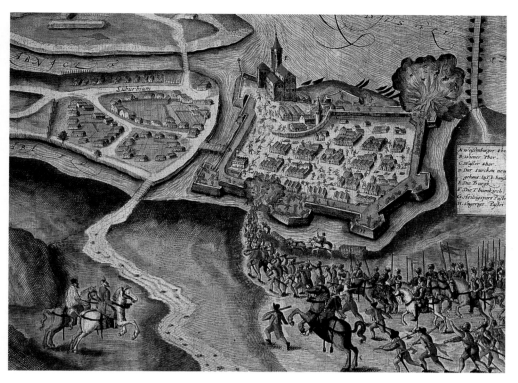

38-39 *The Battle of Lepanto in a commemorative 17th-century painting. On October 7, 1571 the Turkish fleet was routed by the allied nations of the Holy League.*

39 top The Hapsburg empire was the European power that had to face the brunt of Ottoman expansionism. The Austrians were often defeated, but also scored decisive victories that put an end to the threat of the Muslims overruning Europe. This 17th-century print shows the city of Raab, which was reconquered by the Hapsburgs.

39 bottom An 18th-century print in the Stapleton Collection with a view of Constantinople, which at that time had already become Istanbul, with its forest of towers and minarets, mosque domes, the Golden Horn, and the city walls.

From the 18th century on, painters, men of letters and travelers went to Istanbul to find inspiration for their works. Orientalism began to become popular: the fascination of the *harem*, the voluptuousness and luxury, the gorgeous dress, the incomprehensible language and writing, the perfumes and veils–all this titillated the undocumented fantasy of those who wrote descriptions, which were often romanticized, of the age-old lifestyle of a country that was simply different.

Further and further removed from the government which had by then fallen into the hands of courtiers, eunuchs and concubines, the sultans frequently granted European agents the right to run and exploit various sectors of the Ottoman Empire's economy. This series of delegations of authority, known as treaties of capitulation, entrusted the tobacco and cotton industries, the postal and railway systems, and almost all the vital areas of the economy to foreigners, and the

CONSTANTINOPOLI

my. The sultans reacted to the country's increasing adversities with almost masochistic indifference; the only one who seemed to be interested was Mahmud II, who at least solved the problem of the Janissaries in drastic fashion: he had them shot to death. The sultan also made some reforms that met with stiff resistance in the elephantine bureaucratic system. Among the public works worthy of note were

sultan thereby forfeited their right to act personally on behalf of their country in the sectors most crucial to its well-being, thus giving the Turkish people the impression that only Europeans were capable of being managers and entrepreneurs. This lack of commitment made the European powers think that the Ottoman Empire had become a powerless giant. Therefore, the czar of Russia decided to occupy the Crimea and northern region of

the Black Sea in 1854. Great Britain, France and Italy went to the aid of Turkey, but in vain, since the territories had already been lost and were later annexed by the Moscow government, to which Bessarabia had already been ceded in 1812.

In 1829 the Sublime Porte was forced to recognize the autonomy of Greece, which became a full-fledged independent monarchy in 1832. Moldavia and Wallachia followed suit, while Egypt came under the British sphere of influence. The empire's economy also went into an inexorable decline, so much so that in 1881 the state declared bankruptcy and Turkey officially became Europe's sick econo-

the two bridges erected in the heart of Istanbul on the Golden Horn, the Galata and Unkapani bridges.

In the meantime, the middle class, which had slowly developed, had put its hopes in progressive receptiveness to innovation in the person of Midhat Pasha, a politician who had been grand vizier for a short time and was quite influential in the sultan's court. When the very young sultan Abd al-Hamid II was crowned in 1876, Midhat managed to persuade him to promulgate a constitution. This major event was intended as the first step toward some form of democracy, but the sultan abrogated the constitution as soon as it was promulgated.

40 top These views of the Sultanahmet and Süleymaniye mosques by the 19th-century French painter Flandin evoke the fascination of Istanbul.

40 center The incredible jumble of domes and buttresses in Hagia Sophia towers over the houses of Istanbul in this 19th-century view.

40 bottom The sinister figures seen here are Janissaries (yeniçeri in Turkish), members of the elite corps of the Ottoman infantry.

41 The interior of Hagia Sophia, illuminated by evocative shafts of light, is the subject of this fine 1862 lithograph by Gaspare Fossati.

Built in early Byzantine times as a Christian church, the edifice was turned into a mosque by the Ottomans in the 15th century and is now a museum.

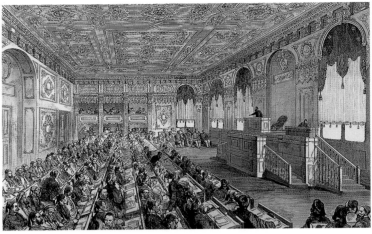

However, Hamid II was not impervious to modernization, since he allowed the construction of roads, railway lines, aqueducts and telegraph lines and also promoted industry. In 1888 the Paris-Istanbul railway line, the fabulous Orient Express, was inaugurated with a great deal of pomp and ceremony; this train soon became a legend, attracting adventurers, diplomats, simple travelers in search of adventure, aristocrats, ballet dancers, and profiteers. The East and Europe thus drew closer together. And in order to accommodate visitors to Istanbul, the luxurious Pera Palace hotel, which now attracts curiosity seekers, was built. But the Ottoman Empire continued to fall to pieces as Crete, Bulgaria, Armenia and Macedonia broke free from Turkish dominion.

The early 1900s witnessed the foundation of the Young Turks movement, which in 1908 had a new constitution approved. The following year the Young Turks forced Parliament to depose Abd al-Hamid for incompetence, and he was replaced on the throne of the Sublime Porte by his brother Mehmet (or Muhammad) V, a faint-hearted person who was nicknamed Vahdettin. The new sultan took his brother's place so that a triumvirate of members of the Young Turks group could in effect rule the country. The three–Talata, Enver and Cemal–certainly had valid liberal ideas on how to put things right, but in 1914, at the outbreak of the First World War, they made the fatal mistake of siding with Germany, albeit half-heartedly.

The Turkish army had been weakened by the recent campaign in Libya against Italy, which had won the war, as well as by the continuous battles it had to wage against Russia, which, on the eastern frontier of the country, persisted in its attacks and gained important positions and areas in territories inhabited mostly by Armenians, who relentlessly opposed Ottoman rule. This negative scene was relieved only by a moment of glory in 1915, during the battle of Gallipoli on the Dardenelles.

42 bottom right
In 1912 Turkey was involved in the Balkan War and two years later made the unfortunate choice of taking sides with Germany in World War I.

42-43 After the Young Turks' coup, Istanbul and the entire country witnessed a series of riots and revolts in the streets. This photograph was taken in front of the Sublime Porte of the Topkapi Palace on January 23, 1913.

43 bottom left
A historic photograph of some of the leaders of the coup that deposed the sultan, Abd al-Hamid, in 1913. From left to right, Mahmud Sevket, the new Grand Vizier, Enver Bey, and Izzet Pasha.

43 bottom right
The sultan Abd al-Hamid, the last sovereign who actually ruled in Turkey, was deposed in 1909 by the Young Turks movement and died in prison in 1918.

*44 top
November 1918 at
Istanbul: the
commander of the
Allied forces lands on
the shores of the
Bosporus to organize
the headquarters of
the occupying troops.*

*44-45 The last
action of the
European Allies
offensive against
Turkey was the
entrance of British
troops in Istanbul in
1918.*

The Turkish troops were headed by Mustafa Kemal, the future Atatürk, who did battle with the Allied army, consisting of British and French troops and Australian and New Zealander battalions. The Allies were certain of victory and had already made plans on how to partition what remained of the Ottoman Empire, but the crushing defeat at Gallipoli was a sobering lesson in humility.

In any case, the Turks were forced to agree to a humbling armistice, which was signed at Mudros in 1918, and only the shadow of the former

45 top The beach
and the Seddul Bahr
field in the southern
area of Gallipoli,
photographed in 1915
from the bridge of the
HMS River Clyde,
which was part of the
French-British fleet
sent to fight in the
bloody campaign for
possession of the
peninsula.

immense Ottoman Empire remained. The Allied powers' plan to dismember the empire was as follows: Iraq and Palestine would go to Great Britain, Syria and Lebanon would become a French mandate, Italy would get the Dodecanese Islands in the Aegean Sea, while Istanbul itself would be put under Russian control. In the meantime, along the coastline, Greece persisted in her dream of the "Great Idea," based on the reconstruction of what had been Hellenic territory in ancient Asia Minor. For the moment, the Greeks had already gained the city of Smyrna and the region of Thrace. Never before had Turkey been so close to disappearing from the map of Europe and the Middle East. It was then that Mustafa Kemal decided to act decisively to save his country.

The occupation of Smyrna by the Greeks in May 1919 was the last straw for Kemal. The reigning sultan, Muhammad VI, was a puppet and certainly was no obstacle. In 1920 Kemal convened the National Assembly at Ankara which approved his project and gave him the power to enact it. The future Atatürk thus began to organize the War of Independence. First he forced the Georgians and Armenians to return to their territory in Russia; then it was the Italians' turn, as

45 bottom The cover of the piano score of *"The Siege of Constantinople,"* an event which in reality never occurred thanks to the campaign in the Gallipoli peninsula in the Dardenelles Strait, in which the Turkish troops kept the Allied forces at bay.

last sultan, Muhammad VI, fled from Istanbul and the following year the Turkish Republic was proclaimed and recognized internationally. The first president was Mustafa Kemal Atatürk. A weighty task awaited the "father of modern Turkey": he had to lead his country into the 20th century. He took a path that was drastic and did not admit of any dissension, certain as he was that the only way to lead Turkey into the modern world was to abandon the models of the past for good.

First of all, he made Ankara the capital of Turkey because it lay more in the heart of the country than peripheric Istanbul. Then he abolished Arabic script and imposed the Latin alphabet for the Turkish language, prescribed the Gregorian calendar and prohibited the fez, the traditional Ottoman headdress. Women were forbidden to cover their faces with veils and were granted the right to vote and to be elected; Islamic law was replaced by non-theocratic laws; polygamy was forbidden; and lastly, the theological schools were closed. Turkish people were forced by the law to choose a last name, which they never had before. After many ups and

they had to leave the islands and other areas ceded to them. The next step was to repulse the Greeks, who by then had already attacked the interior of the country. The battle at Sakarya was decisive, as it forced the enemy troops to retreat, which was followed by the capture of Smyrna by Kemal on September 9, 1922. The Greeks who had been residents of Turkey for generations were obliged to leave their homes and return to a country that they found difficult to call their own, and the same fate awaited the Turks living in the Salonica region in Greece, who moved to Turkey.

Because of the serious disagreement concerning the best way to face these profound upheavals, Atatürk announced that the centuries-old Ottoman Empire was a thing of the past and had to be abolished. In 1922, the

46 top Born in 1881, Mustafa Kemal, seen here as a young man, was later given the surname Atatürk, or "Father of the Turks."

46 bottom The Ottoman delegate signs the Sèvres peace treaty (1920), in which the partition of what remained of the Ottoman Empire was sanctioned. This treaty was not accepted by the Turkish Republic.

46-47 In May 1919 the Greeks occupied the city of Smyrna (now Izmir), which had a large Greek community. Atatürk's troops besieged the city and recaptured it on September 9, 1922.

downs, incredible difficulty and severe economic measures, Turkey made great progress. To a large degree Atatürk ignored the free enterprise system and favored a sort of planned economy, with a drastic reduction of foreign capital and importation.

The death of Atatürk in 1938 was a terrible blow for Turkey: this statesman was idolized, to say the least, partly because he himself had led an austere lifestyle and had dedicated himself wholly to the interests of his country. He was succeeded by Ismet Inönü, who had been his advisor and faithful friend from the war years to the government period. Inönü had the great virtue of not imitating Atatürk while at the same time pursuing his aims, the first of which was to keep Turkey out of World War

Two. Thus the nation created by Atatürk remained neutral until 1945, when it relented to international pressure and declared war on Germany as a mere formality. That same year Turkey was made a member of the United Nations.

47 center In 1924, free elections on a "one man, one vote" basis were held to elect the Turkish National Assembly. This photo shows a polling station in Istanbul.

47 bottom Atatürk decided that women should also have the right to education. Here is a group of women students at the Women's Professional School in Istanbul.

The only political party with any power was the Republican People's Party, while other groups were severely controlled, even though in a short time movements grew up to protest the lack of true opposition parties in Turkey. After 27 years of uninterrupted power, the Republican People's Party was defeated in the 1950 elections by Celal Bayar, who had founded the Democratic Party together with Adnan Menderes, who became prime minister.

Turkey intensified its relations with the United States, which gave her considerable amounts of money in aid, asking in return the right to set up military bases on Turkish territory, a proposal unpopular with the political left. Although the economy had begun to produce a certain degree of national well-being, Menderes was accused of not allowing opposition and of governing the country despotically, which led the army to overturn his government in 1960. Menderes was tried for betraying the Constitution and was subsequently executed. General Cemal Gürsel, one of the leaders of the coup d'état, had a new constitution drawn up with more progressive principles.

This period witnessed the birth of the first Turkish Socialist Party and the Democratic Party changed its

48 top Ismet Inönü, Mustafa Kemal Atatürk's right-hand man, inherited the great statesman's ideological and moral principles, replacing the "Father of the Turks" after his premature death at age 57 in 1938.

48 bottom The leader of the Democratic Party, Adnan Menderes, seen here with Celal Bayar.

48-49 Necmettin Erbakan, leader of the conservative Salvation Party, exults with his thumb up in sign of victory in the 1995 elections.

49 right Tansu Ciller, an economics expert, became prime minister in 1993, the first woman to hold such a high office in Turkey.

name, becoming the Justice Party, headed by a person who has been a leading political figure in Turkey since then, Süleyman Demirel. In 1963 free elections were held and the government consisted of a coalition of conservatives and nationalists, while the following elections were won by Demirel and his party.

However, the economy languished and inflation, the eternal enemy of the Turkish finance ministers, was soaring. Furthermore, the strife between the left wing and right wing worsened to such a degree that the army stepped in with yet another coup. Parliament was reopened in 1972, and the new prime minister was Bulent Ecevit of the Republican People's Party, which did not discriminate against Muslims. In 1974 Ecevit sent troops to the northern part of Cyprus to protect the Turkish Cypriots and prevent the Greek-Cypri-

Nevertheless, even on a practical level, Turkey is a surprising country. It marks a rare case on the world scenario at the turn of the 21st century: time and again the country has boasted respectable economic growth, thanks to the success of a rapidly expanding private sector, as well as the development of the electronics and automotive industries.

On the other hand, traditional agriculture has continued to absorb 35% of the population, slowing down the development of other sectors, above all in areas such as Anatolia.

At the same time, a key sector – the textile industry – has faced increasingly greater pressure from international competitors. In any event, the situation in the first few years of the 21st century has proven to be quite promising.

In 2005 inflation reached the lowest level in 30 years, and foreign

ots from effecting a coup that aimed at making the island part of Greece. The Turkish Republic of Northern Cyprus was proclaimed unilaterally, but has never been recognized by any nation except Turkey, and the Cyprus question is still one of the burning debates in the Mediterranean area.

After the landing of Turkish troops in Cyprus, there was a series of government crises in Ankara and no end to the skirmishes among the political parties and the guerrilla warfare between advocates of the left and right wings. The situation became extremely serious, so once again the army led by General Kenen Evren intervened, suspending civil rights and parliamentary activity. A National Security Council was established, ruling the country with an iron hand and thus further alienating Turkey from the community of democratic nations,

which had already condemned the invasion of Cyprus. In 1983 the Turkish Army allowed free elections, which were won by the Motherland Party, headed by Turgut Özal, an economics expert. Özal proved to be a dynamic prime minister who fostered free enterprise, a move that fostered the economic boom that lasted through the 1980s. In 1989 he was elected President of the Republic.

Following Özal's death in 1993, a woman held the post of Prime Minister for the first time in Turkish history, reflecting a groundbreaking change. Tansu Ciller, an economist, continued the promising path of privatization undertaken by Özal. Despite all her efforts, however, inflation and devaluation continued to increase, triggering serious financial crises in the country in 1994, 1999 and 2001.

investors have shown growing interest in this country, which is determined to become more and more modern.

On a cultural level in particular, Turkey – led by Istanbul, considered one of the world's trendiest cities – is gradually regaining the role it lost following World War I. The world is looking to this country with admiration and is enchanted by its countless attractions. All this has helped open the "gateway to the East" towards a new reality that looks ahead to the future, but without destroying its priceless heritage.

THE THOUSAND FACETS OF TURKEY

50 bottom right
The interior of the Ülu Camii, or Great Mosque, at Bursa, is decorated with a lovely grey marble fountain the water of which gushes out on three levels. The mosque was built in 1379 and has a 328 feet perimeter and 20 domes. Verses from the Koran in archaic Arabic are on the piers.

50-51 Vast sunflower fields descend softly onto the shores of the Dardanelles. Not far from this peaceful rural area lay the city celebrated by Homer, Troy.

51 top left
Thrace boasts one of the masterpieces of the Turkish architect Sinan, who designed the most beautiful Ottoman mosques: the Selimiye Camii at Edirne, an

architectural jewel in the last strip of Europe, which is part of Turkey.

51 top right In the eastern region of Turkey, not far from the Syrian border, the scenery is at times rather barren. This is a view of the land near Malatya, a short distance from the solitary mausoleum of Antiochus I on the Nemrut Dag mountain.

50 left The first architectural masterpiece one sees upon arriving in Turkey from the west is the Selimiye Mosque at Edirne.

50 center right The Mosque of Murad II at Bursa was built in 1426. Its garden houses 13 türbe, funerary chapels for the sultans. The central sarcophagus belongs to Murad himself, who wanted it placed under the opening in the middle of the dome so that the rain would fall on it.

*T*urkiye'ye os, geldiniz (welcome to Turkey), an extraordinary country that alternates metropolises like Istanbul and deserted steppes; spellbinding stretches of blue sea and coast and fields of wheat, tobacco and cotton; and mountains covered with forests where bears and wolves live.

Our brief survey of the regions of Turkey begins with the least-known one, Thrace, the last strip of the Balkans, which ends magnificently at Istanbul, on the Bosporus. The reason for this stopover in Thrace is ancient Adrianopolis (now Edirne), which is rich in 15th-16th century mosques and boasts a masterpiece of Ottoman religious architecture, the splendid Selimiye Camii, or "Mosque of Selim," which was designed by Sinan, the great architect of the Sublime Porte's golden age. Built on a rise in 1557 for Sultan Selim II, this majestic mosque dominates the city with its four sharply-tapered minarets. The interior, which is illuminated by light filtering through 999 windows, is a masterwork of decoration with its Iznik majolica and sculpted marble.

Just southeast of Istanbul on the Sea of Marmara, is the Gulf of Izmit, which has many wooded rises and vast olive groves that supplied the sultans' table with oil. Going around the gulf to the west, is the city of Bursa, the capital of the Ottoman Empire until 1416. It stands on the slopes of Ulu Dag (8343 feet) and was much appreciated by the ancient Romans, who exploited the local hot springs. The old city counts 125 mosques and the tombs of the sultans Osman and Orkhan, while modern, industrialized Bursa has outshone the fame of Iznik, ancient Nicaea, known for its ceramics. Wide paved roads penetrate the flat Anatolian plateau, touching Gordium and the mystery of its tumulus: a royal tomb found intact that may belong to King Midas.

Not far away is Ankara, the new capital that was Atatürk's dream, much like a European metropolis. At the double wall of the 3rd century B.C. Galatian citadel that dominates the multicolored wooden houses in the old town, the extraordinary Museum of Anatolian Civilizations, located in a han, or indoor marketplace, offers a picture of the journey made by man in this area of its very origins. The city also has the remains of an Ionian temple built in the 2nd century B.C. which was later dedicated to Augustus when the province was taken over by the Romans. A modern monument in the capital is the square and austere Mausoleum of Atatürk.

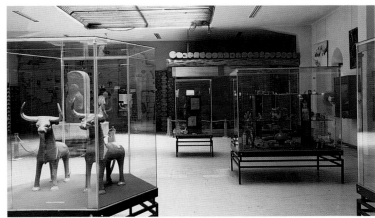

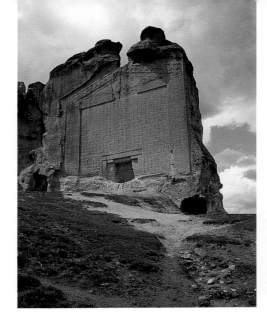

Proceeding eastward, one comes to Bogazköy, ancient Hattushash, the massive Hittite capital. Together with the remains of the Great Temple, dedicated to Hatti, the god of the elements, and the sun goddess Arinna and perhaps the largest edifice in the world during the heyday of the Hittites, the Royal Gate and the Lion Gate give one an idea of the vastness of this city. In fact, Hattushash was the much-feared capital of an empire extended over all of Turkey and beyond, as far as Cyprus and the Aegean Sea, and then sank into oblivion. However, it is the city walls that testify to the grandiosity of Hattushash, since they are so massive that the Greeks, five centuries after the fall of the Hittite empire, thought they were the work of a race of giants.

A short distance away, the land protects the natural passageways of the rock-cut sanctuary of Yazilikaya, decorated in the 13th century B.C. with magnificent bas-reliefs portraying Hittite gods and sovereigns. Standing out among the former is Teshup, the storm god who was a major deity of this bellicose population. Here lies the most ancient heart of Turkey, among yellowish plains delimited by mountains dotted with groups of tents belonging to the *yörük*, the nomad shepherds and carpet weavers who are becoming rarer and rarer. The cultivated fields burst with unexpected colors: the white cotton, dark green tobacco plants and yellow sunflowers paint landscapes that have remained unchanged for millennia.

54 top left
The rather low terrain around Bögazkale becomes fairly high ground at Yazilikaya, near the impressive ruins of Hattushash. This site, which in antiquity was inhabited by the Phrygians and was known as the "Abode of Midas," houses the 6th-century B.C. rock-cut tomb seen in this photograph. It is named after the same king.

54 top right
The galleries in the rock-cut sanctuary at Yazilikaya extend into a rocky outcrop a short distance from the Hittite capital of Hattushash. The route taken by visitors among the openings between rock faces in this site, sacred to the people who lived here three millennia ago, is studded with series of bas-reliefs portraying divinities and sovereigns.

54-55 The Lion Gate, which has the same name as the monumental entrance at Mycenae in Greece, gives access to the ruins of this ancient capital with warlike traditions. Monumental architecture was not a Hittite monopoly, but in the case of Hattushash it astonished even the Greeks, who were certainly not new to such amazing cities.

55 top right Besides its slowly developing industry, including tourism, the main activity in Turkey is still agriculture, thanks to the vastness of cultivable land. Sunflowers (or helianthus), which can be seen everywhere, beginning with the Balkan region, provide oil which is appreciated for its lack of harmful fats.

55 center and bottom right The area around Hattushash lies in a region that is rather isolated from the developments that are transforming Turkey. The only changes made in the age-old local agriculture are the new products—tobacco, cotton and sunflowers—and the great increase in the extension of the crops. This solitary nomad and the three women picking cotton do not seem to be affected by the fact that their country is making every effort to become integrated into the European Union.

Kayseri, ancient Caesarea Mazaca, is the gate to Cappadocia and a leading cultural center with mosques and theological schools whose fame dates back to the 13th century. This city is dominated by the Erciyes Dagi volcano, whose eruptions have created the geological miracle of this region.

Cappadocia comprises a lunar landscape of lava shaped by thousands of years of erosion that has offered shelter to shepherds, hermits and monks and is now one of the most popular Turkish marvels with visitors. The eerie pinnacles known as "the Fairies' Chimneys," the caves, needles and gorges in this magical, unreal scenery has no equal in the entire world.

The Christian monks who lived in Cappadocia during the rise of their religion cut chapels out of the soft tufa and in their intense, primitive style painted delicate frescos that the fury of iconoclasts damaged and partly destroyed. Fortunately, what has remained is enough to enchant visitors who still come to the churches of Cappadocia under the hieratic yet benevolent glance of Christ Pantocrator, the "Almighty," painted inside the domes. For many months every year the best-known villages–Göreme, Avanos and Ürgüp–are filled with tourists, but only a short distance away there is a virtually unknown Cappadocia which includes Soganli and the Ihlara Valley, localities rich in rock-cut, frescoed chapels and churches standing solitary and almost forgotten in a primeval

landscape. Cappadocia is fascinating not only for its unique landscape and archaeological treasures, but also for the archaic life of the local farmers, who only very recently have been forced to abandon their dwellings cut out of the tufa.

A short detour southwest takes us to the area in Turkey most dedicated to orthodox Islam, at Konya, 31 miles from the very ancient archaeological site of Catal Hüyük, one of the first cities in the world.

One of the primary reasons for a visit here is the Mevlana Tekkesi, a convent for dervishes–the Islamic monastic fraternity founded by Jalad ad-Din Sumi whose members attained a state of ecstasy through whirling bodily movements during the *sema*, a ceremony that is still held, albeit without any religious meaning. Another attraction is this holy man's splendid mausoleum (*türbe*), designed in brilliant green tiles that make the monument visible from any part of the city. Another surprise in store for visitors to this fabulously beautiful region are the astounding localities of Kaymakli and Derinkuyu, which are mentioned by Xenophon in his *Anabasis* (or *Persian Expedition*): two huge cities cut out of the bowels of the earth to serve as refuges from the many devastating invasions, places that literally make one dizzy. The Kaymakli complex, which was perhaps already inhabited in the 5th century B.C., is articulated on different levels. A surprising feature of

58-59 Cappadocia has amazing landscapes such as this, where it seems impossible that fruit trees could grow.

59 top left Üçhisar ends in a rock whose peak offers a view of the entire region. It is the custom for people to come here to admire the sunset.

59 center right In 1925 Atatürk closed the convent of the Whirling Dervishes, but on the feast day of its founder, the Persian Sumi, the dizzying sema is still danced.

59 bottom right The türbe of the Mevalana Mausoleum is a magnificent symbol for Konya: its color seems to allude to the tolerance preached by the Persian mystic.

61 top left The style
of the churches in
Cappadocia is
Byzantine, with
Armenian and
Syrian influences.
Here we see a fresco in
St. John's at Göreme.

61 top right
The interior of the
beautiful church at
Kadir Durmus has no
frescos but still has the
pulpit and elegant
arches that divide it
into two sections.

this "ant heap" hewn out of the earth
by Man are the furnishings in the
rock-cut chambers–benches, tables,
and beds, all cut out of the soft tufa.
Derinkuyu is even larger. Consisting
of seven superposed levels, this rock-
cut city covers a surface area of 1.5
square miles and could take in thousands of persons in its countless
chambers, which were connected by a
network of galleries.

60 top left The fine
frescoes in the church
at Çavusin reflect a
synthetic style that
distinguishes it from
the other chapels in
this area.

60 top right
The "Hidden
Church," thus named
because it was cut out
of the rock and of
difficult access, is at
Göreme and has well
preserved frescoes,
thanks to the dry
climate.

60-61 St. John's
Church, or Yusuf
Koç, at Göreme is an
extraordinary edifice
cut out of the tufa in
the 9th-10th centuries
A.D. The
characteristic of the
inner chambers is the
play of domes, arches
and sections of
columns.

61 center right
The two most
important
underground cities in
Cappadocia are
Kaymakli and
Derinkuyu. This is a
view of the labyrinth
of passageways in the
former town,
discovered in 1963,
consisting of seven
levels where the local
populations
presumedly took
shelter in wartime
and during raids by
warlike nomads.

61 bottom right
The perfectly
organized life in the
underground cities
allowed thousands of
persons to live in the
bowels of this region.
Each level is a little
less than 9.8 feet high,
and the passageways
descend as much as
246 feet.

The immense region of eastern Turkey revolves around Lake Van, a small, inland sea on a scorched plateau surrounded by the Upper Taurus Mountains, which are covered with snow for months, and by unbounded, half-desertic spaces abounding in castles and caravanserais. Over the centuries, many transhumant populations of different origin settled on the shores of the lake, 5577 feet above sea level. The last to arrive were the Afghan-Kirghiz, descendants of Genghis Khan who struck roots in Altınçay after being driven out of Pakistan. Today they live here in an environment like the one in the country they had to abandon, and still wear their traditional dress.

Since prehistoric times many different ethnic groups have found refuge in this land where the Tigris and Euphrates begin their course. According to legend this was the region where the Garden of Eden stood before the Deluge, while archaeologists state that around the 8th century B.C. the city of Van (ancient Tuspa) was the capital of the Urartu kingdom.

There are many castles in the Van region, from the Urartian fortress of Çavustepe to the massive fort, built in the 17th century, that dominates the city of Hosap, about 37 miles east of Van, and the impressive fort on the ancient acropolis of the city. In the large lake is an island with the magnificent Armenian church in the Akdamar monastery, built in the 10th century, now visited by few tourists.

64 top In 1881 a German engineer, Karl Sester, garnered information from a Turkish geologist and told the world about this forgotten marvel amid the rugged mountains of eastern Anatolia: the Mausoleum of Antiochus I of Commagene, which dominates the region.

64-65 The mysterious, timeless and disturbing colossal heads scattered over the terraces of the mausoleum on the top of Mt. Nemrut are still awe-inspiring despite the fact that the statues bearing these huge heads have been reduced to rubble over the centuries.

65 top left After a cold night on the Anatolian mountains, the dawn sun warms the head of an eagle on the eastern terrace of Mt. Nemrut.

65 top right and center These faces portray the goddess Tyche and, perhaps, the megalomaniacal occupant of the mausoleum, Antiochus I.

West of Van and the city of Di-yarbakır, on the top of Nemrut Dag (7388 feet), are the mysterious ruins of the Mausoleum of Antiochus I, the son of Seleucus I and king of Commagene, the small region along the upper course of the Euphrates river. The summit of this impressive mountain, the tallest in the region, is flanked by two immense terraces, one facing east and the other west, built by Antiochus

The colossal heads and the fragments of bas-reliefs on the top of the mountain tell the story of a visionary and megalomaniac king who built his immense tomb, forgotten for over two millenia until a Turkish geologist discovered it a century ago.

around 62 B.C. These two open spaces are surrounded by colossal heads about the height of a man, which belonged to the statues of the Greco-Roman divinities worshipped at Antioch–Apollo, Tyche, Herakles and Zeus–which the king claimed were his ancestors. One-day excursions to the summit of Nemrut Dag are organized in the town of Katha, about 62 miles from the slopes of the mountain.

It often happens that in books on Turkey the northern region of the country is mentioned only briefly, quite unjustly, because the Black Sea coast has many surprises in store for visitors. These are the waters that led the Greek troops–which had disbanded after the ill-fated battles against the Persians described by Xenophon in his *Persian Expedition*–to shout, "*Thalassa*!" (the sea!). From Sile to Hopa the 745.6 miles of coastline pass by interrupted here and there by non-descript towns and villages once inhabited by fishermen and farmers and now filled with new, commonplace houses, many of them still unfinished.

However, not human activity but nature stands out here, where the Pontics mountains descend to the water, sometimes softly and at other times precipitously. On these mountain slopes, where tobacco, tea, fruit and cereals are cultivated, at harvest time the colors of the earth blend in with the bright blues of the women's dress. The green and wild interior is clothed in conifer forests crossed by rushing torrents and inhabited by abundant fauna. The sea fills the fishermen's nets with *hamsi*, the sardines that are cooked in 101 different ways.

This is the region of ancient Greek Colchis, the land of the people the Romans called Lazones, with light-colored eyes and blond hair. Trabzon (Trebizond), a very ancient and lively city, boasts an acropolis with St. Sophia Church, built in the 13th century, which is known for its fine Byzantine paintings.

66 top left and right
The colorful fish markets in the towns along the coast of the Black Sea, which has innumerable fish. These two photographs reveal the charm of Zonguldak, northwest of Ankara, one of the principal towns on this coastline together with Sinop (ancient Sinope) and Trabazon (Trebizond), which the Greeks called Trapezus.

66-67 The Corub torrent flows peacefully in the valley it was named after, flanked by rows of poplars and cypresses that add a gentle touch of green to an otherwise barren landscape.

67 top left
The Sumela monastery is perched on a dizzying rock face, and most of it is rock-hewn. The first settlement in this inaccessible site was founded by the hermits Barnabas and Sophronius (4th century A.D.), who hid an icon of St. Luke here.

67 right The precious frescos at Sumela somehow escaped the vandalism that took place in the monastery in 1923 after the Greek monks left it.

The proximity of Russia makes Trabzon a merchandise sorting center and a city given over to traffic of every kind, not all of it legal. The gem of this region is the Virgin of the Black Mountain Monastery at Sumela, perched on a steep cliff overlooking a forest, as unreal and isolated as the Meteora monasteries in central Greece. The buildings we see today are from the 12th century on and were enlarged to house hundreds of monks, the last of which lived here until 1923. The frescoes decorating the churches and chapels of the monastery are of exceptional artistic worth and, like the rest of the complex, are in urgent need of restoration.

68 top left
An Anatolian farmer woman is protected from the cold by her brightly colored clothes. Mt. Ararat (17,500 feet), always covered with snow, is in the background. Tradition has it that Noah's Ark ran aground on this mountain when the Deluge subsided.

The Turkish landscape becomes even more secluded southeast of the Black Sea, in the region occupied in ancient times by the Urartu kingdom, which flourished in the 9th-7th century B.C. This area is dominated by Mt. Ararat, the biblical peak on which Noah's Ark presumedly ran aground and is now the massive natural boundary between Turkey, Iran and Armenia.

Agri Dagi, the Turkish name of this famous mountain, is a volcano rising 17,500 feet above sea level, an immense cone that bewitches mountaineers as well as that special category of explorers who are perhaps dreamers, since they insist on searching for the legendary Ark.

From a geographic and geological standpoint, Mt. Ararat consists of two volcanic cones separated by a very wide saddle that are called "Great Ararat" and "Little Ararat"; the first is dormant and the latter has been extinct for thousands of years.

Divided by the present-day Russian-Turkish border, the ruins of the ghost city of Ani (Ocakci) are one of the most exciting, and neglected, sites in eastern Turkey. Beautiful churches in solitary splendor amid the tall grass, half-ruined ramparts, and rubble are all that remains of the former capital of Armenia, which around the year 1000 had a population of 100,000 and about one thousand religious buildings that were doomed to oblivion by earthquakes, invasions and fires.

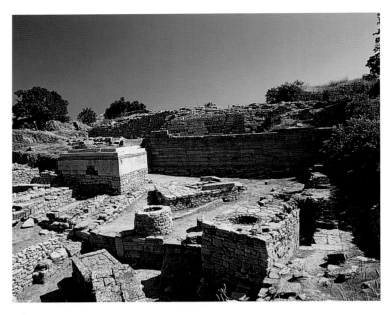

70 top left *Troy was destroyed and rebuilt many times, which explains the origin of the nine city levels identified by archaeologists. This is a view of the sacred precinct at Troy VIII and Troy IX (ca. 700 B.C.-300 A.D.).*

70 center left The most significant ruins in Troy are undoubtedly the walls of the various city levels. The section of wall seen here has been dated at 1700-1250 B.C., the period that probably ended with the siege by the Achaeans, recounted by Homer.

70 bottom left One of the best preserved monuments in Troy is the small odeon outside the city walls, the construction of which (400-350 B.C.) reveals its Hellenic origin.

70-71 The coastline of the ancient kingdom of Lycia abounds in views such as this one. Small, sandy inlets alternate with others characterized by white boulders washed by the sea, and everywhere the crystal-clear water has turquoise and emerald-green hues.

71 top left In order not to disappoint visitors' expectations of something clearly "Homeric" at Troy, a wooden Trojan horse has been placed at the entrance to the site in tribute to the epic poem par excellence, The Iliad, which narrates the exciting and tragic siege of this great city.

71 top right The clock tower is a monument that Çanakkale is proud of its clock-tower monumento. This city owes a lot to the proximity of the world-famous ruins of Troy, but for centuries it has been important mainly because of its strategic position at the mouth of the Dardenelles.

The coast of the huge Asiatic region of Turkey, divided between the Aegean and Mediterranean, begins from the Dardanelles and ends at the Orontes River on the Syrian border. This extremely long coastline virtually originates at one of the most famous cities in the ancient world, Troy, which was brought to light by an adventurous amateur archaeologist called Schliemann who, certain he would find the legendary city of Priam, in 1871 began to excavate the Hissarlik mound facing the Dardenelles, near present-day Çanakkale. His intution proved to be exact, and Troy, along with some of its treasures, was brought back to life.

The following digs by German archaeologists, which were better organized, showed that the city Schliemann had discovered was really one of nine successive cities that occupied the Hissarlik mound over the centuries from the Bronze Age to the Hellenistic and Roman periods. Experts later ascertained that the city razed to the ground by the Achaeans was probably Troy VII, which, as is only logical after being sacked and destroyed by fire, yielded very few finds. Therefore, besides the echoes of Homer, there is very little in Troy that illustrates the myth of the heroes on both sides who inspired the dreams of generations of romantics.

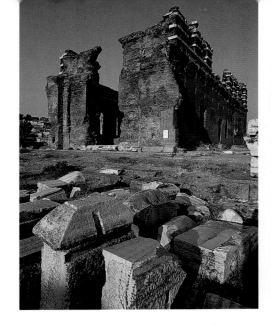

72 top left The Red
Basilica at Pergamum
is an impressive
building whose
function is unknown.
It was constructed in
the 2nd century A.D.,
during Hadrian's
rule, and may have
been the Temple of
Asclepius or Serapis.

72 top right
Pergamum was one of
the most splendid cities
in ancient Asia Minor.
Here we see the Temple
of Trajan, on the
acropolis, the highest
part of the city.

South of Çanakkale are other archaeological gems of the Lydian interior–Pergamum and Sardis, cities with flourishing economies and a cultural life that made them famous throughout the ancient world.

Pergamum lies 984 feet above modern Bergama, which is known for its knotted carpets. The golden age of this ancient city began in the Hellenistic age, when it became an illustrious commercial and intellectual center; for example, the city library had over 200,000 volumes and became legendary, ranking second only to the one in Alexandria. The ruins of the theater are quite impressive as well, built on the steep ridge that now towers over the modern-day town. The acropolis area or upper city offers a panoramic view of the Lydian interior and also has notable ruins, as it was the site of numerous temples, among which is the massive and well-preserved Corinthian order edifice dedicated to Trajan, known as the Red Basilica because of the color of the brick that was once dressed with marble.

Sardis was the capital of Lydia and the city of Croesus, the fabulously rich ruler who vied with Midas in luxury and opulence; the magnificence of this semimythical king can be seen in the archaeological precinct, which abounds in grandiose ruins. The so-called Marble Court–the spacious peristyle that gave access to the gymnasium, considered a masterpiece of

72-73 The theater at Pergamum lies on a steep hill and was one of the largest in antiquity; it could seat 10,000 spectators on its 80 rows of tiers and was famous for its perfect acoustics.

73 top left
The incomparably elegant Marble Courtyard is the most precious treasure in Sardis. It was the entrance to the Roman gymnasium (3rd century A.D.).

73 center right
The Romans added great architectural works to the already splendid Sardis. The spacious architecture and white marble are the characteristic features of the entire monument area.

73 bottom right
Among the ruins of the synagogue annexed to the gymnasium is the altar decorated with eagles, lions and fine mosaics.

Severan-age Roman "Baroque"–immediately strikes visitors with the purity of its lines. The ruins of the synagogue next to the baths complex is also noteworthy. Inside is an altar that, curiously enough, is decorated with eagles, a clear-cut violation of Jewish law, which forbade the creation of anthropomorphic or zoomorphic figures, as they were considered idols that might undermine faith.

75 center right
Floral motifs
surround the Medusa
on the lunette over
the entrance to the
Temple of Hadrian,
one of the monuments
on the so-called
Marble Street.

75 bottom right
Emperor Hadrian
often visited the
Turkish coasts and
led military
campaigns in the
interior. His victories
brought about the

construction of many
monuments in his
honor. The section of
the portico
illustrated here
belongs to the Temple
of Hadrian at
Ephesus.

*74 The Celsus
Library at Ephesus
dates from 135 A.D.
and represents the
zenith of Hellenistic
culture. The finest
bas-reliefs that
decorated it are now
on exhibit at the
Kunsthistorisches
Museum, Vienna.*

*75 Top left In the
ancient Greek cities
the agora was a
square surrounded by
arcades in which
commercial
transactions, political
discussions and
simple conversations
took place. The agora
at Ephesus seen in this
photograph, was one
of the largest in the
world–360 feet long.*

*75 Bottom left
The odeon at Ephesus
lies toward the
beginning of the
"Marble Street." This
edifice, which had a
seating capacity of
1,400 and was
donated to the city by
P. Antoninus Vedius
in the name of his
wife Flavia Papiana,
was probably dressed
in wood.*

Then there are Izmir, a megalopolis on the Mediterranean coast which, thanks to its status as a port, has become truly cosmopolitan, and Kusadasi, a lively seaside resort with a view of the Greek islands of Chios and Samos that has grown to excess because of its proximity to the magnificent city of Ephesus.

A visit here means experiencing the thrill of "discovering" archaeology because of the impressive ruins of a city with material and spiritual riches that was destined to become one of the most important parts of the huge Roman Empire. Very little remains of the Temple of Artemis, one of the Seven Wonders of the Ancient World, but in the heart of ancient Ephesus there are baths, fountains, monumental buildings, columns, temples and theaters built of marble that are almost perfectly preserved. In the archaeological precinct the formal purity of buildings such as the Celsus Library, the façade of which alone is testimony of the splendor of ancient Ephesus, and the Temple of Hadrian, contrast with the majesty of the theater with a seating capacity of 24,000, a huge *cavea* that offers visitors the spectacle of white ruins that dot the rises and the street which once led to the port and which looks like a marble ribbon stretched over the plain.

76 top The Temple of Apollo at Didyma, one of the most famous sanctuaries in the ancient world, measures 390 by 197 feet, while the 122 columns that supported the structure were 63.5 feet high. Its construction went on for centuries, from the 3rd century B.C. to the Roman period, but even this was not sufficient, as the temple remained unfinished.

76-77 The large theater at Ephesus faces the paved street that once led to the port, which is now silted up. This grandiose edifice of Hellenistic origin was rebuilt by the Romans from 41 to 117 A.D. The cavea could seat 25,000 persons and was originally 98.5 feet high.

77 top left This impressive marble face of Medusa once decorated the architrave of the Temple of Apollo at Didyma. The land around the temple still has fragments of architectural elements, but the finest ones are now on display at the British Museum, London.

77 top right After losing access to the sea because of the lowered sea level, the city of Priene was moved to a rocky spur. Despite the dramatic circumstances that necessitated this move, it put the city in an exceptionally lovely location.

77 center left On this marble element, which is part of the Gate of Herakles in Ephesus, the mythical hero is portrayed dressed in the pelt of the Nemean lion which he killed. The ruins in the background line the Street of the Curetes, which was destroyed by an earthquake in the 4th century B.C. and immediately rebuilt. The Curetes were priests from Crete who officiated the cult of the young Zeus at Ephesus.

77 bottom left The theater at Miletus, partly hewn out of a small hill and supported by a massive buttress wall, was built at the entrance to the city and overlooked the port, which no longer exists. The first row of tiers of this impressive construction, which had a seating capacity equal to that of the theater in Ephesus, has some inscriptions with the names or titles of the persons for whom the seats were reserved.

Beyond Kusadasi the coast is flat and sandy, with small, deep gulfs and a hinterland dotted with fascinating ancient Greek cities, archaeological gems of rare beauty situated in the alluvial plain created by the winding Maeander (Menderes) River.

The first one on this route, perched in an exceptionally beautiful location on a craggy spur, is the Ionic city of Priene, designed in the 5th century B.C. by Hippodamus of Miletus in a rigorous grid layout. The main monuments on this site are the Temple of Athena Polias, with its Ionic columns, which was donated to the city by Alexander the Great, and a small Hellenistic theater, which has a sacrificial altar of the Dionysian cult.

Just southward is Miletus, of Mycaenean origin, which during the classical age became the most important city in the Ionian League. The magnificent theater in this city is simply astounding for its size and state of preservation. It dates back to the 4th century B.C. and was enlarged to its present size by the Romans in the 2nd century A.D.

In ancient times a paved road led from Miletus to the city of Didyma, celebrated for the huge oracular temple of Apollo. This never-completed edifice was supported by massive columns and made of equally huge marble slabs, one of which weighs 48 tons. The famous marble relief portraying the Medusa has become almost a symbol of Ionian culture.

78 top left A tomb in the necropolis of Hierapolis emerges from the ground covered with crystallized limescale from the Pamukkale hot springs. This water does not obstruct plant life.

78 center left The city of Hierapolis grew up because of the therapeutic hot springs in the area. The king of Pergamum, Eumenes II, decided

to found the city in 190 B.C. The Romans beautified and enlarged it, building among other things the large theater seen here.

78 bottom left The north gate of Hierapolis was built during Emperor Domitian's reign. The accessway led to a wide porticoed street paved with marble and lined with workshops and houses.

78-79 This blinding landscape, of an almost surreal white, consists of terraces filled with very calcareous petrified water. At Pamukkale, which, not surprsingly, means "Cotton Castle," are the hot springs that create this extraordinary environment of immobile, petrified falls.

Making a detour from the coast toward the east, in the rural interior we arrive at the white pools of Pamukkale, a geological marvel created by the extremely calcareous spring water, which forms basins and white stalactites, limescale formations that stand out against the dark slopes of the mountain. From a distance Pamukkale, the "cotton castle," looks like a fortress as white as the cotton in the nearby fields. The hot springs in this area were already famous in antiquity for their therapeutic properties, especially for curing skin and eye diseases and forms of rheumatism. Next to the falls is the large ancient Roman city of Hierapolis, a site known for its baths that was razed to the ground by an earthquake in 17 A.D. and then revived until the 3rd century. The site has outstanding ruins, and even in the bottom of the pools with their milk-white water, one catches a glimpse of remains of columns and capitals that belonged to the ancient baths.

79 top left The pool at the Pamukkale Hotel is really a Roman bath, on the bottom of which are fragments of columns and capitals that fell after one of the many earthquakes that destroyed Hierapolis, the Roman city next to the petrified terraces.

79 top right Another enthralling view of the baths at Pamukkale. Until a few years ago people were allowed to swim in the natural pools that formed in the travertine ledges of the hill. But when this natural marvel began to deteriorate and become dark, the government prohibited swimming.

Among the cotton fields of a verdant agricultural zone in the Anatolian interior is Aphrodisias, the city of the sacred love rites, which was inhabited as early as the Bronze Age and dedicated to the cult of the goddess Aphrodite during the Greek and Roman periods. Today this very ancient site welcomes visitors with two surprises: the magnificent theater, which in the 2nd century A.D. was transformed into an arena for gladitorial contests; and the ruins of the stadium, which in ancient times had a seating capacity of 30,000 and is one of the most interesting Greco-Roman monuments in the world. The ruins of the Baths of Hadrian are also impressive; they are flanked by the remains of the gymnasium and the Temple of Aphrodite,

which the Byzantines turned into a Christian basilica, many columns of which are still intact. Aphrodisias, rediscovered in the early 20th century, has many decorative statues that bear witness to the existence of a local sculpture workshop whose works were appreciated and exported throughout the Roman Empire many are now preserved at the local museum.

80 Smooth, tortile and fluted columns support the Tetrapylon at Aphrodisias, a short distance from the ruins of the temple of the goddess the city was named after.

81 center left and bottom left The remains of a small odeon (above) and a view of the portico of Tiberius, which once housed offices and workshops.

81 top right and top center right Overall view and detail of the skene of the theater, which is still used for cultural events.

81 bottom center right and bottom right Aphrodisias has formidable ruins of buildings used for entertainment. Besides the remains of the theater, there are the impressive stadium (above) and most of the odeon.

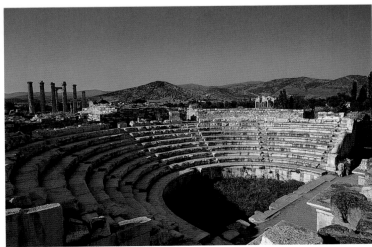

82 top left The castle dominating Bodrum has an interesting museum with archaeological finds recovered from the sea. Today this city is a lively and important tourist resort. Nothing remains of the tomb of king Mausolus–one of the Seven Wonders of the World.

82 top right St. Peter's Castle was divided into several sections occupied by the Crusader knights from different countries. In the photograph is the German Tower in the foreground, the French one at left, and the Italian one at right, half-hidden by the vegetation.

The modern, fashionable town of Bodrum lies around the Crusader fortress that dominates the port, St. Peter's Castle, built by the Knights Hospitalers from Rhodes in the early 15th century. This was ancient Halicarnassus, and the mausoleum of its king Mausolus of Caria was one Seven Wonders of the Ancient World. This astounding edifice was commissioned by Artemisia, the wife of the the Persian satrap, in the 4th century B.C., but now only a few stones remain. In fact this magnificent monument, intact until the 12th century A.D., shared the lot of so many other ancient works, as it was demolished so that its stones could be used as building material, in particular for St. Peter's Castle.

The deep Gulf of Gököva (or Kos) separates Bodrum from Marmaris, together with the thin, meandering peninsula dotted with villages such as Datça; here beaches and bends alternate as far as the ruins of Cnidus, a veritable Eden for lovers of ancient ruins and the landmark between the Aegean and the Mediterranean. Marmaris was beautiful and boasted a temple dedicated to Aphrodite, with her statue sculpted by Praxiteles, that later disappeared. Today the only testimony is the Ottoman fortress that dominates the promontory. In fact, just like Bodrum, Marmaris is basically a famous and popular tourist resort which marks the beginning of that part of the stretch of coastline known as the Turquoise Coast, which ends at Antalya and its gulf.

82-83 The port of the lively town of Bodrum is dominated by the Crusader St. Peter's Castle. The town lies over the site of ancient Halicarnassus, which is famous for the monumental tomb that Artemisia built in honor of her husband Mausolus, the satrap of Caria, which was part of the Persian Empire.

83 top Marmaris, another popular tourist locality, has an active port, hotels and restaurants, and is always quite lively. Only a small and partly rebuilt medieval castle bears witness to the long history of this town.

83 top right, center right and bottom right The Gulf of Marmaris (above) is surrounded by vegetation. The entire peninsula that extends beyond the town (center and bottom, two views of its port) is a succession of roadsteads, beaches and delightful corners with very few towns. The pine groves descend to the shore and the sea is unpolluted.

84 top left
The reddish rock faces in the last stretch of coast of the Taurus Mts. are dotted with rock-hewn tombs. The ones seen here are in the Myra necropolis, near the town of Demre, which according to legend is the birthplace of St. Nicholas, or Santa Claus.

84 center left
The rock-cut tombs at Kaunos tower over the Kirenis River, not far from the sea. The inhabitants of the ancient city went down in history for their sickly appearance: they were decimated by malaria, which was quite common in this marshy area.

84 bottom left
A Lycian sarcophagus with its characteristic pointed top supported by four pillars: this is the classic Lycian tomb for persons of rank.

84 top right
The entire coastal region of ancient Lycia is studded with rock-cut necropolises, but the complex of Fethiye, ancient Termossos, which was hewn out of a barren cliff, is certainly the most spectacular one. The tombs here are a mixture of eastern and Hellenistic influences.

84-85 and 85 top right In the large Gulf of Fethiye there is an almost labyrinthine series of hidden roadsteads and inlets that can be reached only by boat. For those who love the sea this is a paradise of sun and tranquillity.

85 top left
The magnificent Tomb of Aminta carved out of the reddish rock of Fethiye around 350 B.C., is modelled after an Ionic temple. The frieze below the tympanum is particularly beautiful.

About 31 miles east of Marmaris is Kaunos, with the ruins of a theater of clearly Greek origin, a Corinthian temple, and Roman baths. But the most interesting feature of this locality are the rock-cut tombs, which date from the 4th century B.C., the façades of which stand directly over the sea. Tombs similar to these are also to be found at Fethiye, which in ancient times was known as Telmessos and was the most important city in Lycia. Unfortunately, many ancient ruins here were damaged by two quakes in 1956 and 1957, but fortunately the rock-cut tombs, which date back to the 6th-3rd century B.C. and are considered among the most beautiful in the region, were not destroyed. The best preserved of these, known as Aminta's Tomb, dominates with its splendid façade *in antis*, that is, a façade supported by two columns with Ionic capitals that are inserted between two anta pilasters.

Just past Fethiye is an area rich in history. In rapid succession there are Letoon, a city dedicated to Leto, the mother of Apollo and Artemis, with the remains of three temples dedicated to these gods; then Xanthus, which boasts a series of cuspidal sarcophagi supported by tall columns and decorated with extremely lovely bas-reliefs, and a Roman theater; and lastly, Myra, with a rock-hewn necropolis whose marvelous tombs are crowded together on a craggy rock face.

87 bottom left
Antalya was protected by thick walls, of which only a few towers and section remain. This photograph shows the Hidirlik tower, built in Roman times to be used as a lighthouse.

87 top right
The Diden River flows into the sea near Antalya in the form of a violent waterfall that drops over the cliffs.

87 bottom right
The pure lines and color of the mausoleum of Zincir Kiran Mehmet Bey at Antalya remind one of certain architecture in Central Asia, where the ancestors of the modern Turks lived before conquering territories to the west and founding a huge and powerful empire.

Ölü Deniz, the most photographed beach in Turkey, lies here–the gateway to the animated seaside villages of Kalkan and Kas. An elegant, vivacious town, Kas has a picturesque old section that is famed for its production of hand-made fabrics and faces one of the most beautiful bays on the Turquoise Coast, right opposite the Greek island of Kastellorizon. Proceeding northward along

86 top left There are many craftmen's shops and fish restaurants on the narrow streets of Kas.

86 top right Opposite Kas and its gulf, only a few kilometers from the coast, is Kastellorizon, the easternmost Greek island.

the coast, one arrives at Antalya, a large city that has the most interesting archaeological museum in the region, with a fine collection of Lycian, Hellenistic and Roman statues. The town also has an old yacht harbor surrounded by wooden Ottoman houses, some of which have been turned into hotels, and flanked to the east by the Hidirlik tower, a Roman lighthouse used in the Middle Ages for defensive purposes. Another fine sight not far from Antalya is the picturesque Diden river falls, which flows directly into the sea.

86-87 Nowadays the small harbor of Kas has more yachts than fishing boats.

87 top left Antalya has become a rather large town, but it still has a perfectly intact small harbor constructed by the Romans during Hadrian's reign (2nd century A.D.). The surrounding quarter has lovely wooden Ottoman houses.

Amazement is the first feeling one has upon entering the theater at Aspendos. This masterpiece of Roman architecture made the fame of this city, one of the most important in ancient Pamphylia, which was rich thanks to the production and sale of salt and olive oil and lovely carpets with spun gold. Aspendos, near modern Antalya, is an archaeological site that is extremely popular with tourists. And by far the major attraction here is the theater; in fact, Kemal Atatürk was so enthralled by it that he had it restored to perfection so that it could become the venue for spectacles and concerts. The skene, or permanent scenic construction behind the orchestra, is perfectly preserved, though it lacks the marble slab facing it had in ancient times; the tiers opposite it could easily seat 15,000 spectators.

Now we head east, 8 miles from Antalya, to Perga, a major Hellenistic cultural and trade center that was very prosperous. The locals claimed they were descendants of Calchas and Mopsus, two soothsayers who fled from burning Troy and came all the way here. Perga was conquered without a struggle by Alexander the Great and stretched to the foot of a hill that now houses the remains of the Byzantine acropolis. The theater, cut out of a hillside, still has some marble panels with bas-reliefs that decorated the skene with portraits of Dionysus. Next to the theater is a beautiful oval stadium which in ancient times had a seating capacity of 15,000. The city baths, among the finest in all the archaeological sites in Turkey, have the usual series of chambers–*calidarium*, *tepidarium*, *frigidarium*, *apodyterium*, etc.–the pavements and basins of which are faced with marble slabs. It should be added that most of the statues kept in the museum of Antalya come from Perga.

88 Top and bottom left In the fertile land behind Antalya are the ruins of the aqueduct of Aspendos, an example of the architectural and engineering skill of the Romans. Tiberius Claudius Italicus had this aqueduct built. One of its bridges was 2789 feet long, and there are still remains of the towers that regulated the flow of the water.

88-89 The theater at Aspendos is the most outstanding monument that this formerly active and flourishing city has left us. Instead of being cut out of a hill, it was supported by massive walling that determined its height and diameter. The wonderfully preserved cavea could seat 15,000 persons.

The flat coastline beyond Antalya penetrates ancient Cilicia, which is dotted with Ottoman and Crusader castles and was the domain of unbelievably cunning pirates. Here, where the water is warmer, Hellenistic ruins such as those at Side crop up from the sandy shores, alternating in grotesque fashion with large modern hotels. The sea washes the ruins of this city, which in Anatolian dialect was called "Pomegranate," the fruit that symbolizes fertility. The mouth of the Eurymedon River is not far away.

Side was founded in the 7th century B.C. by Aeolian colonists, and was later easily conquered by Alexander the Great; after his death it was ruled by the Seleucids of Pergamum, becoming a major trading port that the Romans later exploited. The city began to decline in the 12th century A.D. The archaeological area, which is partly surrounded by walls, begins with a section of an aqueduct, which is followed by the ruins of the most important monument in Side, the theater. This is a singular structure because, instead of being cut out of a hillside, as was the custom, it lies against a massive wall that supports the *cavea*, or tiers of seats. The orchestra basin, which was fed by nine canals, was quickly flooded for the *naumachiae*, the extremely popular naval battles that were represented in theaters during the Roman period.

96 center and bottom left, top right
96 center and bottom left, top right The museum at Alanya (center left) counts many Hellenistic mosaics and Roman statues. At top right is a mosaic from Samandagi (2nd-3rd century A.D.) with Bacchus and Adriadne dancing, while at bottom left is a detail of the 2nd century-B.C. mosaic dedicated to the Four Seasons, from Daphne (today's Herbiye).

Alanya, a favorite haunt of the restless Cleopatra, is now one of the tourist localities in the region with the best facilities. The modern city extends to the foot of massive fortifications built during the Byzantine age, surrounded by walls five miles long that in the past had fifty towers. Our itinerary now takes us toward the Syrian border, through Anamur, Mersin, Iskenderun (ancient Alexandretta or "Little Alexandria"), and lastly, Antakya, called Antioch in antiquity, the city that exudes Levantine fascination and boasts a fine archaeological museum.

96-97 The Alanya fortress is protected by an exceptionally long enclosure wall built by the Seljuks, who furnished it with fifty towers, some of which no longer exist. The first one, the octagonal Kizil Kule or Red Tower, is at the port; it was built in the 13th century and owes its name to its ferrous blocks and bricks.

97 top left Alanya has become a popular seaside resort frequented by tourists from Northern Europe for the most part, who often go there in the winter as well. The long beach is lined with hotels and bathing establishments.

97 top right In the past the area enclosed by the crenellated walls of Alanya was a lively district, but few people have remained in the oldest part of this city, which has preserved its quaint atmosphere.

*98 top left
Archaeologists and
diggers are hard at
work during the final
hours of excavation
at Zeugma, trying to
salvage what they can
from the imminent
inundation of the
site, which is near the
town of Belkis, in
southeastern Turkey.*

*98 top right
The spectacular
Roman mosaics at
Zeugma have yet to
be studied and
classified, since
archaeologists were
forced to salvage them
at breakneck speed.*

Throughout Turkey there are countless vestiges of the past, but very few of them have been given due attention and recognition and have been the object of excavations. There is also an indefinite, but certainly large, number of sites yet to be explored. Among these is Zeugma, whose invaluable treasures were brought to light and then immediately left in the bosom of the earth. It is pointless to look for the name of this locality on maps or in art history books, because Zeugma is a place buried in the distant past, sunk into oblivion, forgotten by legend, disowned by past and present history.

This site lies in an area that was recently flooded as a result of the construction of a large dam near Birecik and Belkis, two small towns in southern Turkey. The Turkish government's irrevocable decision to go ahead with this project triggered a river. This marked the birth of Zeugma, which in ancient Greek means "junction." The city grew and then in the 1st century A.D. the Romans set up the headquarters of the IV Scythian Legion there, the most important Roman military outpost in the Middle East. Later on Zeugma became a stopping point in the Silk Road and had a population of 60,000 (not counting the 10,000 soldiers barracked there). Prosperous for many centuries, the city rapidly declined the sacking and destruction by the Sassanid Persians and never revived. In fact, its name is not to be found in any historic chronicle; however, its memory will be preserved by the marvelous mosaics that archaeologists managed to salvage from the ravages of time and from the recent man-made flood.

Only a few miles away from this lost city is Syria, where another world begins.

race against time on the part of archaeologists. They began excavating frenetically, bringing to light the centuries-old secrets of the existence of this city since the 3rd century B.C., when on the shores of the Euphrates, not far from the present-day Syrian border, King Seleucus Nicator decided to build a bridge over this large

*98-99 An intense
gaze from the depths
of the past. This
detail is from one of
the Roman mosaics
at Zeugma, now on
temporary exhibit at
the Archaeological
Museum of
Gaziantep, a few
miles from Syria.*

*99 center
The refined
workmanship of the
mosaics at Zeugma
should come as no
surprise. This locality,
which to us seems so
distant from Rome,
was for the Romans
just another place to
be beautified with art
works and
monuments, as if it
were the capital itself.*

*99 bottom
The flooding of the
site was postponed
several times, but
when the order was
finally given, it took
only three weeks for
the Euphrates River
to cover Zeugma
forever.*

ISTANBUL: GATEWAY TO THE ORIENT

100 top left
The characteristic wooden houses at Üsküdar on the Asian shore of the Bosporus were recently restored. They are dominated by the walls of the Anadolu Hisar (Fort of Anatolia).

100 center left
The bold span of the first bridge on the Bosporus crowns the white Beylerbeyi Palace in the background, one of the last royal residences the sultans had built in "European style" in the 19th century.

According to such a disenchanted traveler as Mark Twain, one should arrive at Instanbul by sea, sailing through the dark waters of the Sea of Marmara to enter the bottle-neck of the Bosporus and to see on its two banks the towering minarets and domes on the mosques, the ultra-modern and audacious bridges, the skyscrapers, the centuries old Topkapi palace, and the labyrinth of piers. In fact, the natural accessway to the very soul of Istanbul has always been the sea.

Never as in the 20th century had the Turkish metropolis witnessed such a social, political and cultural mixture and fusion of Near East and West. Striking contrasts are to be seen in the outskirts, which take in newcomers from the countryside and where Islamic law and religious feeling is stronger and more tangible, while in the residential neighborhoods of the Bosporus there is a European atmosphere and the restaurants serve raki, the national aniseed liqueur.

Massive urbanization has drastically altered the borders of Istanbul. Districts as large as cities have grown up in every direction, often without rigorous town plans; the Asian area of Üsküdar has grown immeasurably, and European Istanbul is literally spreading like wildfire. According to the latest estimates, the city has more than twelve million inhabitants.

Times change here with dizzying speed, but for visitors the first glimpse of the Orient begins in the historic center, where the city of many names originated: Byzantium, Constantinople, Istanbul.

From a topographical standpoint, the complex urban layout is divided by the Bosporus into two large sections, which are now joined by two bridges as well as by ferries that depart and arrive from the piers of Eminönü. The European section is in turn divided by the long Golden Horn inlet, which is crossed by three bridges (the outermost one is the famous Galata Bridge). Istanbul therefore really comprises three sections, not to speak of the series of delightful villages on the north shore of the Bosporus that are rapidly becoming urbanized.

The historic-monumental core of Istanbul is Sultanahmet, the rise where both the mythical and chronological history of the city began: from the arrival of the Greek king Byzas, the mythical founder of the city, to the tragic love of Hero and Leander; from Roman dominion to Constantine's bold decision to make it the new capital of the empire; and from the splendor and decadence of the Ottoman Empire to the rise of Atatürk.

102 top left These
characteristic domes
rise above the harem
of the Topkapi Palace,
which was not only a
luxurious prison
where the sultan's
women were
confined, but also
included the sultan's
usual living quarters.
As many as 300
women lived in the
palace.

102 top right
An austere arcade
delimits a courtyard
in the harem area.
Intrigues, coups and
barbarous crimes were
planned and carried
out in the secrecy of the
harem, where the
women were often the
power behind the
throne.

102-103 This lovely
panoramic view of
Istanbul also shows us
the extension of the
Topkapi Saray

complex, the sultan's
palace built on a rise
dominating the city
and the Bosporus.

103 center left
A fountain with three
basins in front of the
Sultan Ahmed II
Library is richly
adorned with friezes
and calligraphic
decoration. Water was
always extremely
important for the
Ottomans, who had fine
fountains built
throughout their empire.

Our journey of discovery in Istanbul begins with the Topkapi Saray, the seat of the Sublime Porte, the magnificent palace complex which for centuries was the residence of dominating and inept sultans alike, whose lives were divided between bloody court intrigues and luxurious confinement in the *harem*. In front of the main entrance to the palace, is the foreboding polygonal fountain where the Janissaries cleaned their blood-stained scimitars after executions. Nowadays there is nothing macabre about this pavilion; on the contrary, it is an introduction to a microcosm filled with marvels. This palace, half of which is a bare residence and the other half a museum, is a hotchpotch of different

103 top right
In spring the flower
beds around the
Topkapi Saray are
filled with tulips (lale
in Turkish), which
the sultans loved. The
bulbs were stolen and
secretly taken to
Europe.

103 center right
The Sultan Ahmed II
Library, built in
1718 for this ruler,
who loved art and
literature, now houses
an extremely fine
collection of precious
imperial clothes and
costumes.

103 bottom right
Besides being the
sultan's residence, the
Topkapi Saray was
also the administrative
seat of the Ottoman
territories. Here we
see one of the pavilions
where the sultans
granted audiences.

104 top left
The middle of the large terrace next to the Baghdad Pavilion is occupied by one of the many fountains that decorated the Topkapi Saray. The balustrade, interrupted by a gilded kiosk, has a panoramic view of Istanbul and the Bosporus.

104 center left
The Topkapi palace consists of many cloistered courtyards, almost all of which have extremely well-kept gardens. The first such courtyard was occupied by the elite Janissary corps, who had a great influence on court affairs and often caused the rise or fall of sultans.

104 bottom left
Beyond the elegant portico seen here is the Hirka-i-Saadet, or Apartment of Happiness, a series of rooms for distinguished visitors, furnished with precious furniture and Iznik tile decoration on the walls.

104-105 One of the largest and most luxurious pavilions in the Topkapi Palace houses the Imperial Treasure, a collection of jewels, gold and silver necklaces, jade, pearls, diamonds, rubies and emeralds that the sultans ordered from all over the world to decorate daggers, rings and crowns. The famous Topkapi diamond, which is not cut, is also kept here.

105 top left and right
Naturally, the most luxurious parts of the Topkapi Palace were the sultan's private apartments and the staterooms, but even the size of the kitchens show quite clearly that this complex was a veritable city within a city. The former service rooms are now used to house the fine collections of ceramics and porcelain.

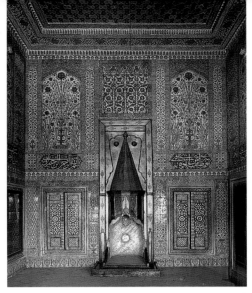

106 The word "divan" derived from the Turkish diwan, which was the assembly of the leading authorities, who laid down state policy and elaborated the most important laws. This photo shows one of the audience halls with a luxurious baldachin where the participants were received.

107 top left Every detail of the Topkapi Palace shows modern-day visitors the astounding luxury and wealth that characterized the life of the sultans. It is easy to understand why the European diplomats and visitors who were received at the Istanbul court of Istanbul were so impressed.

107 center left In the middle of this polygonal hall with an arabesqued dome is a magnificent bronze brazier placed on a beautiful rug. All the doors and windows were covered with wooden panels with slits so that those inside could look outside without being seen.

styles divided into four large court-yards and surrounded by walls, ter-races and gardens that tower over the city. From the courtyard of the fright-ful Janissaries one passes to the heart of the palace with the government ad-ministration chambers, the kitchens and the *harem*, which in reality was the part of the complex where the sul-tan lived with his family. Visitors see only one-tenth of what was the harem: decorated rooms with Iznik ceramic tiles, marble fountains, courtyards em-bellished with flowerbeds and corners shaded by many species of trees, and baths.

Next are the halls of the Imperial Treasury, which consists of dozens of showcases with jewels and precious stones such as the Kasikçinin Elmasi, an 86-karat diamond, and the emerald that weighs no less than 7 pounds. Often the sultans vied as patrons of the arts to beautify the sumptuous palace with ele-gant works. Interesting examples of this are Ahmed III's library; the halls given over to the exhibition of magnificent collections of clothing, refined fabrics and porcelain; and the armories.

107 bottom left Baskets of fruit and bouquets of flowers decorated the walls of this sumptuous room, which is illuminated and made larger by the play of mirrors. The colorful enamelled panels are further animated by the rows of gilded tesserae.

107 top right A corner of the Baghdad Pavilion: note the arabesqued niches decorated with mother-of-pearl inlay set into the walls covered with tiles with floral trimming. Islamic tradition does not allow representation of the human figure.

107 center right The Circumcision Hall is one of the loveliest in the Topkapi palace. An infinite range of blue hues is set against a white ground that almost disappears under the profuse calligraphic decoration, in which one can recognize parrots and deer.

107 bottom right Detail of the Iznik tile panels that decorate the Circumcision Hall. Tiles are a "poor" material compared to the gold and marble that abound in the Topkapi palace, but the effect they create is of unsurpassable elegance.

108 The famous throne seen here, known as the "Throne of the Feasts," dates back to the 16th century and was used by the sultans only for religious celebrations. It is made of walnut covered with gold leaf, with small rosettes in relief, and once had a baldachin.

109 left This parade helmet covered with damascened gold and decorated with turqouise and rubies, dates back to 1550, the last phase in the reign of Süleyman the Magnificent (1494-1566). Such a richly decorated object obviously could not have had a practical function, but it gives us an idea of how the sultans and warriors were dressed during the golden age of the Ottoman Empire.

109 top right The showcases containing the Topkapi Treasure have this stunning curved dagger with a metal sheath that is studded with diamonds and also has three unusually large emeralds in the handle. One of these latter conceals a tiny watch that dates from the mid-18th century.

109 bottom right This throne with a baldachin was made for the sultan Ahmed I in the early 1600s. It is overwhelmingly lavish, studded with ivory, mother-of-pearl, rock crystal and precious gems that are combined to form the usual naturalistic motifs. The throne is capped by an impalpable rock crystal feather. Hanging from the baldachin are a gold medallion, an emerald and pearls.

110 top left
The flagon in this photograph is literally covered with emeralds and rubies, the sultans' favorite gems. The chasing that connects the stones in gold was done in the 16th century.

110 top right
This flask, which stands on an octagonal base, was made out of a single piece of rock crystal. The spouts on either side are held up by gold chains.

110 bottom All the implements needed to create the sinuous and fascinating calligraphy the sultans loved so much, were contained in this 16th-century oval casket, the outside of

which is entirely covered with emeralds, rock crystal and rubies. This was the fabulous period in which the wealth of the Ottoman Empire rulers probably reached its peak.

111 top left Among the many marvelous objects in the Topkapi Museum, the jewel in this photograph is certainly not overshadowed. Ornaments of this kind were placed on silk turbans as brooches. The harmonious design of this piece–which is made up of diamonds, pearls and gold–makes it look delicate without diminishing its preciousness.

111 top right
The Kasikçi, also known as the "Spoon Merchant" diamond, is of uncertain provenance.

It probably came from India, ended up in the hands of Napoleon's mother, and was then sold to the sultans.

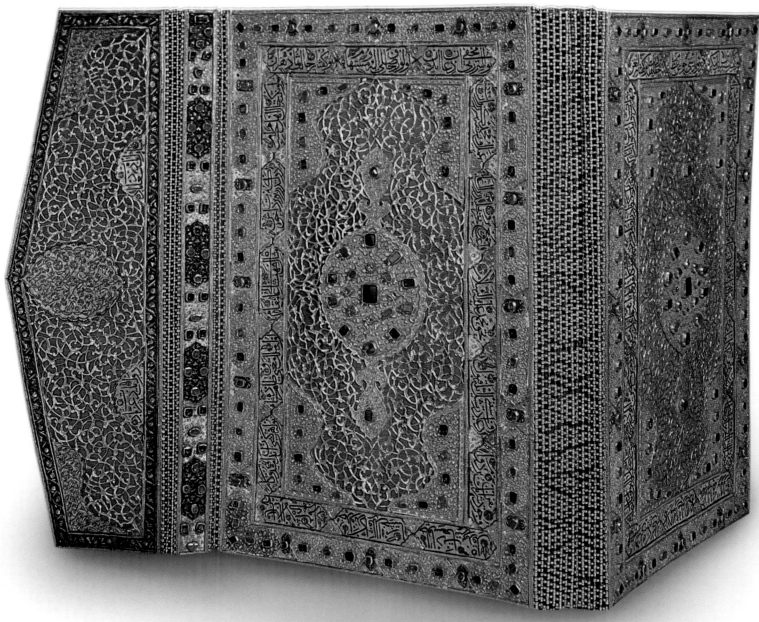

111 bottom Not one inch of this 16th-century book cover is undecorated. The volume belonged to the sultan Murad III and is covered with small semi-precious stones, enamel, gold and meticulously wrought, perfect geometric relief.

112 top left Massive, austere, impressive: this is the exterior of Hagia Sophia seen from the gardens surrounding it. The sheer size of the former church is overwhelming. It is crowned by a huge dome flanked by two half-domes, a typical feature of the architecture of the time.

112 top right This view of Hagia Sophia shows how the massive dome rests on a row of tall, narrow windows and has few apertures. It has a diameter of 102 feet and is 180 feet tall. The church was built over the ruins of the earlier Hagia Sophia destroyed during the violent rebellion of 523 A.D.

112-113 An aerial view of Hagia Sophia, dedicated to Divine Wisdom. It was built during the reign of Justinian the Great and was consecrated in 543 A.D. It was conceived and designed by the architects Anthemius of Tralles and Isidorus of Miletus. Kemal Atatürk had it turned into a museum.

The monumental Hagia Sophia church also lies on this hill. Visitors are awe-struck by the munificence of the Byzantine Christian tradition. It was built in the 6th century by Justinian over the foundations erected two centuries earlier, and throughout the ages suffered collapses, fires and plunder. When the Ottomans arrived in 1453 it was converted into a mosque, and is now a museum. Its unusual, distinctive architecture was the model for St. Mark's Basilica in Venice.

113 top left The play of lines in the dome is clearly seen in this photograph. The portico seen above allowed worshippers to go through the women's galleries. Many marble elements came from ancient monuments; for example, some columns were taken from Ephesus and Baalbek.

113 center left With the advent of Islam many mosaics decorating the Christian churches were destroyed, but most of them were covered with stucco and brickwork. The mosaics in Hagia Sophia portray Christ Pantocrator, the Virgin Mary, the Apostles, and some of the Byzantine emperors.

113 right This view of the interior of Hagia Sophia illustrates the vastness of the building and its overpowering architecture, which is animated by the polychrome marble panels, the galleries and the porticos in the upper section. The pavement we see today is not part of the original building.

The many minor domes that surround the main cupola of Hagia Sophia are elegantly balanced by the six slender minarets on the nearby Mosque of Sultan Ahmed, known as the Blue Mosque because of the color of the fantastic Iznik tiles that decorate the interior. These minarets can be seen from all corners of Istanbul and

are a reminder of the immutable harmony preached by Islam. The mosque also includes a theological school, a canteen, a hospital and a caravanserai.

Almost nothing remains of the Byzantine city except for the Hippodrome, on the tiers of which the "fans" of antiquity went wild during the exciting chariot races. Certainly nothing like the marvelous construction it was then, the oval Hippodrome has only three surviving monuments: the Egyptian obelisk of Tuthmosis III, the Serpentine column from the Sanctuary of Apollo at Delphi, and the Column of Constantine VII. On the other hand, for many centuries the stupendous bronze horses have been missing, since they were stolen by the Crusaders in 1204 and taken to Venice; they are now kept in the museum of St. Mark's Basilica.

115

A series of rolling avenues and small streets lined by wooden Ottoman houses–some of which have become small, charming hotels–and by nondescript condominiums a little worse for wear, lead to the macrocosm of the Kapali Carsi, the Great Bazaar. One of the entrances to this commercial district is next to the Beyazid Mosque, near a small shaded square filled with stalls with antique books. The Bazaar complex is interesting for its arched architecture and galleries, while the shops themselves have lost most of their former Levantine fascination. However, although the carpets and traditional, exquisitely wrought copper, brass and hide products are now mixed with jeans and T-shirts, bargaining still takes a long time and is always accompanied by the ritual glass of *elmali çay*, or apple tea. There are 4,000 shops in all, but the Bazaar also houses mosques, fountains and restaurants.

116 top A crowd of potential customers in the jewelry area of the bazaar in Istanbul. Turkish gold is a little less pure than 18-carat gold and is almost always reddish because it has some copper in it.

116 bottom left A long series of arabeque arcades flanks the Kapali Carsi, or Great Bazaar, which includes restaurants, a café, a post office, banks, the police station and a mosque. This market is open every day from 8:30am to 6:30pm except for Sunday.

116-117 Until a few decades ago the Kapali Carsi was frequented by the citizens of Istanbul, who purchased articles for their everyday needs. Now many products have disappeared and much importance has been attached to Turkish handicrafts and souvenirs, especially carpets.

117 Three scenes of life in the Great Bazaar: top left, a vendor of simit, the salted doughnut-shaped roll with sesame seeds; center and bottom right, the colorful and extremely aromatic Spice (or Egyptian) Market.

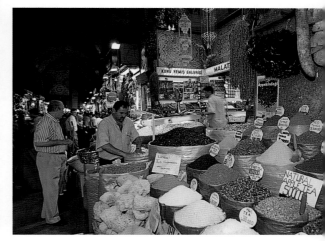

A smaller and cozier marketplace almost opposite the Galata Bridge— where once swarms of boats were moored while their owners sold fresh or freshly fried fish—is the Misir Carsisi, or Egyptian Market, which offers a great variety of spices. Among the large burlap bags filled with scented spices, unusual Galenic remedies, soap, *lokum* sweets, tea, honey, almond sweets and a thousand other things, this market may have a more Levantine flavor.

Nearby is the small, well-proportioned Yeni Camii Mosque. From there a fascinating maze of crowded narrow streets with small shops of all kinds goes up the hill to the large Süleymaniye Mosque, the masterpiece that the court architect Sinan built for Süleyman the Magnificent. The sultan's tomb and that of his favorite wife, Roxelana, are in the back of the structure.

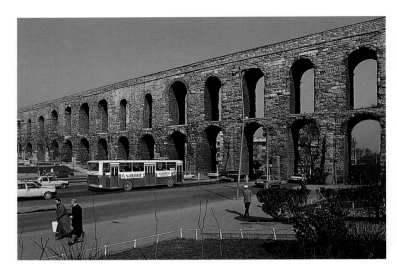

In the vicinity is one of the few ruins from the Roman period, the impressive Aqueduct of the Emperor Valens, which conducted water to the hundreds of underground cisterns in the ancient city, including the fascinating Yerebatan Sarayi (Submerged Palace) basin conceived by the emperor Justinian, which is filled with 336 columns that make it look like a fantastic subterranean temple.

Toward the end of the Golden Horn there is another hill that is a must for visitors to Istanbul: here, in the Eyüp district, is the Eyüp Mosque, dedicated to Muhammad's faithful follower and standard-bearer. It is surrounded by an interesting cemetery with hundreds of tombstones; as is prescribed by the Islamic religion, none of them has any images of the deceased or other decoration except for floral and calligraphic motifs.

122 top left
The beautiful, severe face of Christ Pantocrator seems to be observing the faithful in the exonarthex. For centuries this church was used as a mosque and became a museum when the first restoration work began.

122 top right
Some of the loveliest mosaics are in the exonarthex, the outermost narthex or vestibule in a Byzantine church. Here we see the mosaic under a half-dome depicting scenes from the life of the Virgin Mary.

122-123
The stupendous mosaics in the church-museum of St. Savior in Chora (Kariye Camii) are almost totally intact despite the ravages of the iconoclastic period. The mosaic cycles are considered among the most precious in all Byzantine art both for their great workmanship and motifs.

123 top right
The exonarthex of St. Savior in Chora contains the most outstanding mosaic cycles in the Byzantine world. This vestibule was once used as a mortuary chapel.

The last gem in this part of the city is the St. Savior in Chora church, now the Kariye Museum. The original Byzantine structure erected outside the city walls was converted into a mosque, and was saved from the iconoclasts because the marvelous mosaics and frescos in the interior had been covered. They are the best-preserved Byzantine mosaics in the city, and for those of us who appreciate them in modern times these stunning works mark the height of mosaic production in that age. Besides the representation of Christ Pantocrator (Almighty), characterized by Jesus' right hand blessing the faithful, the panels have episodes from the life of Christ, the Virgin Mary and Adam and Eve.

In the last years of the Ottoman Empire Istanbul expanded to the other side of the Golden Horn, on the Beyoglu hill, where the process of modernization was initiated.

123 bottom right
In the past the church of St. Savior in Chora was at the edge of the city, among fields and vineyards. Next to it there was a monastery complex that was abandoned around 770 A.D., during the reign of Constantine V Copronymus, a fanatical iconoclast.

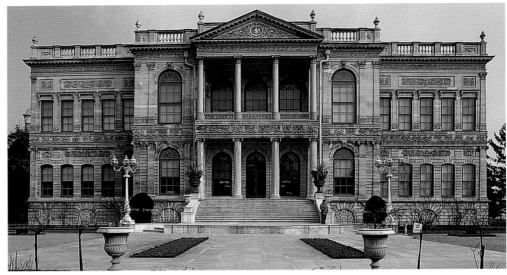

124 top
The construction of the Dolmabahçe Palace marked the definitive move of the Topkapi court to the shores of the Bosporus.

124 top left One of the gates of the Dolmabahçe Palace, which was built along the Bosporus in place of a 17th-century pleasure pavilion. Half a mile railing surrounds the front gardens.

125 top left
The Galata Tower, seen here at sunset, is 459 feet high and was built in the 1300s as a watchtower for the Genoese merchants who lived there.

125 top right
The Serasker Tower, the "Soldier's Head," built by Mahmud II in 1823, housed the War Ministry during the First World War before Ankara became the capital of Turkey.

124 bottom left
The monumental staircase of honor clearly shows that the Sultan Abdülmecit and the architect Balyan used French, Viennese and Italian palaces as their model.

124 bottom right
The construction of the dome of the Throne Room in the palace is a triumph of decorative art. The chandelier in the hall weighs 4.5 tons and can hold 750 candles.

124-125
The Dolmabahçe Palace–here the Throne Room–was built in 1843-56 to testify to Ottoman power and glory, which were really in serious decline.

The Pera, Galata and Taksim quarters bear witness to this with their broad streets flanked by *fin de siècle* buildings. Taksim Square in the evening, with its neon lights and movement, looks like any other metropolis in the world. And all around it are large hotels, the opera house, shops such as those along the Istiklal Caddesi and Cumhuriyet Caddesi boulevards, and the residential areas with their tree-lined avenues. An aperitif at the Pera Palas hotel is not considered trendy, but rather a return to the past to pay due respect to the Istanbul of the *Belle Epoque*. The last sultans, who were so eager to appear to be innovators, abandoned the Topkapi Saray around 1840 and moved to other palaces that were as sumptuous as they were decadent. They had them constructed on the shores of the Bosporus next to *yali*, the wooden summer villas (almost none of which have survived) that belonged to the aristrocrats and wealthy persons from Stambul (the old city on the other shore).

Dolmabahçe, the most magniloquent of these marble palaces, is a mixture of Oriental styles with strong European and Neo-Classic influences. Everything here is immense, glittering and built to dazzle. The throne room is illuminated by a chandelier that weighs 8,800 pound.

But despite all this sumptuousness, the Sultan Abdülaziz decided to build another palace on the Bosporus. He contented himself with Ciragan Palace, only half a mile from Dolmabahçe and its exact replica as regards the mirrors, stuccowork, crystal-glass, friezes and gardens. Most of it was destroyed by arson and it is now a luxury hotel.

On the eastern shore of the Bosporus is the third *fin de siècle* Ottoman palace: Beylerbeyi, built between the edge of the waves and a lovely park. Here again the interior is characterized by *grandeur,* with huge Bohemian candelabra, Sèvres porcelain and carpets.

Other attractions in the outskirts of Istanbul, besides the shores of the Bosporus, are the Adalar, or Princes' Islands, an unusual sight not more than 12 miles south of the city, in the waters of the Bosporus. Büyükada, Heybeliada, Burgaz and Kinali are four islets that were once used as a refuge for ascetics and a place of internment. In more recent times they became summer vacation localities, with villas surrounded by impenetrable walls, a few hotels, and first-rate fish restaurants. There are no automobiles, only *fayton* (one-horse carriages) and bicycles, and the islets have some beautiful beaches and vegetation with a great numer of flowers. Despite being so near to Istanbul, the Adalar are its exact opposite: tiny oases of peace and quiet.

PEOPLES AND TRADITIONS

From the Anatolian farmers to the businessmen in Ankara and Istanbul, the Turks are proud of themselves and their country and have always been united. Sunni Islam is the religion of the vast majority, while a very small percentage of the people belong to various Christian denominations, which causes no problems. Although there has been a certain increase in religious severity in recent times, Turkey is a tolerant country whose search for a stable identity does not allow for excess. Most of the people's attitude toward Islam is based on respect and observance of its laws without resorting to fanatic fundamentalism. However, foreign visitors here should know how to behave in a country with a religion different from theirs: the should take off their shoes before entering a mosque, dress decently, and consume alcoholic beverages with moderation.

The first basic nucleus of the Turkish social pyramid is the family, whose bonds are extremely important. In general Turks are monogamous and the head of the family's wishes are respected. Many marriages are arranged by the couple's parents, although this custom is dying out among the more cultured and Westernized classes.

The stereotype of the dark-haired Turk with a moustache is only partly true, since along the Black Sea coast and in Anatolia one often finds blue-green eyes and blond hair, which are traditionally ascribed to the genes of Alexander the Great's troops.

126 left Although their number has decreased, the groups of nomads in Turkey are still quite common. The largest nomad population is the Yörük group, which refuses subsidies from the government, which is trying to persuade them to settle somewhere.

126 center right This floating fruit market was photographed near Kekova. The greengrocers are really farmers who sell their produce in the villages hidden among the coastal inlets, which are most easily reached by boat.

126 bottom right This woman belongs to the indigenous coastal population of Turkey. Islamic law has not imposed black as the only color for women's dress.

126-127 A family that lives in Diyarbakir. The economy in this region is based on agriculture: its fruit is famous, especially the melons and watermelons, which are even featured in local agricultural festivals held in September.

127 top left Two faces that embody typical Turks: the woman with a snow-white kerchief on her head, and the man, an elderly head of the family, wearing a beret, the modern substitute for the fez, which was abolished by Kemal Atatürk.

127 top right The çayeria is a typical Turkish establishment which serves only different types of tea with varying degrees of sweetness. The leaves come from the intensive cultivation along the Black Sea, as does the apple-flavored tea, elmali çay.

Turkish women are independent and many of them work, sometimes occupying leading positions. At home they are the linchpin of the family and their opinions are given freely and respected. They are hard workers in the fields, in factories, in schools, in offices and in the various branches of handicrafts, especially rug-making, which is a predominantly female activity. *Kilims* and knotted carpets are still made with age-old techniques and patterns that evoke natural phenomena such as rainfall, harvests and fertility. Turkish carpets are always in demand on the international market and are a mainstay of the national economy.

128 top left
The city of Küthaya has replaced Iznik as the leading manufacturer of ceramics and majolica, which are often of excellent quality.

128 top right
The motifs on kilim *rugs, which are mostly geometric, have been found on strips of fabric discovered during excavations in prehistoric Çatal Hüyük.*

128 bottom left
The production of bobbin lace is rather common in Turkey and achieves high levels of workmanship.

128-129 This photograph taken in the Museum of the Turkish Home in Ankara shows a faithful reproduction of the kitchen in the home of a wealthy family a century ago.

129 top right
Cotton picking has always been done by women in Turkey, and only recently have machines been introduced for this work.

129 center right
The masses of cotton fiber that will become yarn or thread are stowed in warehouses before being pressed into balls and then sent to the cotton mills for processing.

129 bottom right
Until a few years ago wool-dyeing was done only with natural colors.

130 top The Turkish bath is a place for meeting friends, exchanging news and opinions, and making business transactions. The baths are open at certain hours for women and at others for men.

130-131 The custom of going to the hammam or public bathhouse to have a vigorous massage is part and parcel of Turkish tradition.

Getting to know Turkey, a truly kaleidoscopic country, by no means consists only of visiting museums, monuments, bazaars and seaside resorts. Turkey abounds in customs, rituals and traditions that are not forbidden for tourists.

For example, the Turkish bath, or *hammam*, is an experience one must not miss. Although with the spread of private bathrooms in modern homes the Turkish bath is not as widespread as it was, it is still an integral part of everyday life that was inherited from the Roman and Byzantine civilizations. The best *hammam* in the large cities were built and decorated with same loving care as the mosques: marble, fine tiles, sculpted fountains, domes, and stained glass.

But what does a Turkish bath consist of? After a long stay in the hot steam, bathers are massaged and rubbed down by the massager, who uses a lot of cold water in the process; then they rest, sipping a glass of tea and chatting with other bathers. Men and women use these baths at different times.

Despite the dominion of soccer, the Turks adore another sport, *Yagli Güres*, or freestyle wrestling, which originated in Thrace. The wrestlers must be bare-chested and put oil on their bodies to make the holds even more difficult. The most popular annual wrestling tournament is held in July at Kirkpinar, with 1,000 participants and hours and hours of elimination bouts.

132 top left
A muezzin calls the faithful to prayer from the top of a minaret. According to Islamic law, worshippers should pray to Allah five times a day.

132 bottom left Worshippers seated inside the mosque in Edirne, one of the masterpieces of the great Ottoman architect Sinan. This photo was taken during the Ramadan, the month in which

the Koran requires that the faithful fast during the day in order to fortify their will-power. In the background are the lovely patterns of Iznik tiles.

132 right A fascinating photograph of the interior of the Blue Mosque in Istanbul. The elegant profile of the minbar, *the tall pulpit used by the* imam *to utter prayers, can be seen in the background.*

Religious holidays in Turkey are, as always, felt deeply and followed by the entire family. The dates vary every year according to the Islamic calendar. The Kurban Bayrami, or Feast of Sacrifice, is as important as Christmas is to us; it is celebrated in memory of Abraham, who, obedient to God's wishes, was about to sacrifice his son Isaac. On this occasion every family "sacrifices" a kid goat and eats it, not neglecting to keep a part of it for the needy. Usually many city dwellers go into the country to celebrate this holiday in the open air. Friends are often invited to participate in the Kurban Bayrami, which is marked by four days of national holiday that usually fall between late spring and early summer.

Ramadan is observed by fasting during the day for 30 days, but this rule is strictly applied only in the most "fundamentalist" areas of the country. The Seker Bayram marks the end of Ramadan and is a three-day national holiday, during which gifts are exchanged and very sweet food is eaten. Needless to say, this is the children's favorite holiday.

Besides national religious holidays, the wedding ceremony is of course a very important event, absorbing families totally in the exchange of visits and gifts. Everything ends on the established day with a huge party that often drains the families' resources.

Turks have loved music since the Ottoman period, when the *mehter*, the Janissaries' Band, sustained vio-

133 The interior of the Süleymaniye Mosque in Istanbul, seen during Friday prayers. Despite Atatürk's promise to make Turkey a secular nation, the

worldwide revival of Islam has also affected this country, where the mosques are again filled with worshippers.

lent battles with loud music. In the past the *asik*, or strolling musicians-story tellers, roamed through Anatolia to entertain villages by playing the *saz*, a stringed instrument, and singing ironic and rather amusing verses. Today, besides the prevailing Western disco music, Turks like the *arabesque*, traditional Turkish music modernized and made topical, in which pleasant melodies are accompanied by lyrics that often have a strong social message.

INDEX

136 At the foot of the tomb of Anthiocus I of Commagene (1st century B.C.), on the top of Mt. Nemrut in eastern Anatolia, is the enigmatic face of Herakles in the early morning sun. By having his own huge mausoleum built, this ruler manifested his desire to be remembered through the ages, but even more, the desire to establish and monumentalize a new theocratic order that would be a sort of fusion of the Hellenistic West and the Persian East.

Map by Michela Auricchio